Human–Computer Interaction Series

Editors-in-Chief

Desney Tan
Microsoft Research, Redmond, WA, USA

Jean Vanderdonckt
Louvain School of Management, Université catholique de Louvain,
Louvain-La-Neuve, Belgium

The Human–Computer Interaction Series, launched in 2004, publishes books that advance the science and technology of developing systems which are effective and satisfying for people in a wide variety of contexts. Titles focus on theoretical perspectives (such as formal approaches drawn from a variety of behavioural sciences), practical approaches (such as techniques for effectively integrating user needs in system development), and social issues (such as the determinants of utility, usability and acceptability).

HCI is a multidisciplinary field and focuses on the human aspects in the development of computer technology. As technology becomes increasingly more pervasive the need to take a human-centred approach in the design and development of computer-based systems becomes ever more important.

Titles published within the Human–Computer Interaction Series are included in Thomson Reuters' Book Citation Index, The DBLP Computer Science Bibliography and The HCI Bibliography.

More information about this series at http://www.springer.com/series/6033

Phil Turner

Imagination + Technology

 Springer

Phil Turner
School of Computing
Edinburgh Napier University
Edinburgh, UK

ISSN 1571-5035   ISSN 2524-4477   (electronic)
Human–Computer Interaction Series
ISBN 978-3-030-37350-4   ISBN 978-3-030-37348-1   (eBook)
https://doi.org/10.1007/978-3-030-37348-1

This Springer imprint is published by the registered company Springer Nature Switzerland AG
The registered company address is: Gewerbestrasse 11, 6330 Cham, Switzerland

Preface

In this book, we pose the question, "Is imagination important to human-computer interaction (HCI)?". While denying such a role is not plausible, the evidence suggests otherwise. There is no substantive treatment of imagination anywhere to be found in the HCI literature. There is no reference to imagination in accounts and models of interaction, or any mention of imagination in any of the popular HCI undergraduate textbooks, and there is little or no mention of it (except obliquely) in the numerous design guidelines distilled from good practice. Yet as HCI professionals, practitioners, researchers, teachers and students, we know that these different expressions of HCI offer a significant role for imagination, for example, we bring to life scenarios or personae with our imaginations and the evaluation of technology typically relies on imaginative "what-if" situations. Perhaps most importantly, we cannot design digital technology without imagination, we cannot use and experience technology without it.

If imagination is as important as we propose, why is there no agreed or generally adopted definition of it within HCI? Well, of course, imagination does pop up from time to time but reference to it tends to be limited to mean creativity. It is as though we have relegated and confined imagination to a supporting role in design.

Perhaps imagination is too exotically psychological to be appreciated by ever-practical HCI? But this is not the case because mainstream psychology itself seems to have little time for it either. There is no established psychology of imagination, and just like HCI, a discussion of imagination is conspicuously absent from textbooks. Even the observation that imagination seems to be a forgotten or neglected feature of our cognition is missing too.

If we want to embrace imagination, perhaps we should confine ourselves to the arts and marvel at the work of da Vinci, but there are simply too many examples of imagination-in-practice in science and technology for it to be ignored, (e.g. Einstein's famous thought experiment which involving him riding (or racing) a light beam). This all stands in sharp contrast this with the view of Vygotsky who regarded imagination to be absolutely foundational of everything human-made, and he is not alone in making such claims. In short, we believe that imagination is central to HCI and this book addresses this hitherto neglected topic.

The Structure of This Book

"Imagination + Technology" is a book of two halves, we begin by defining and understanding the reach of imagination. Most importantly for us is Chap. 2 which identifies the farthings of imagination as mental time travel; supporting the creation of a Theory of Mind; storytelling and creativity. The place of imagination in HCI is explored in Chaps. 3–6.

Chapter 1 Imagination. This chapter sets the scene by briefly surveying how imagination has been treated, and all too often neglected, by psychology and philosophy. We do, however, offer our own definition of imagination based on metaphor.

Chapter 2 We argue that to understand imagination we must focus on how it is applied. We identify and discuss the four key expressions of imagination (the "farthings") which are mental time travel, being able to adopt the perspectives of others (ToM), storytelling and creativity. We also propose that these farthings enable us to be prudent.

Chapter 3 We treat design as making-believe with props (that is, as a form of "thinking with things") where the *props* take the form of probes, sketches and stories. Make-believe is afforded, triggered, scaffolded but constrained by these *props*. Design from this perspective is analogous to pretend play. We also make technology our own, by customising, personalising and making it for ourselves.

Chapter 4 Good and pleasing aesthetics are signs of quality and trust and digital technology is often chosen in the basis of its aesthetics. Here imagination enables us to see the technology as though it were a person and it may be that we assess it as we assess people—that is, quickly, accurately and reliably. This is imagination "seeing as".

Chapter 5 We examine the importance of the imaginary to HCI: we begin with prototyping, then recognise that all digital design still relies on the use of metaphor and all metaphor, in turn, relies on imagination to work. Imagination also allows us to anticipate the experience of technology and to use imaginary technology for real. We end by wondering why there is no mention of imagination in virtual reality.

Chapter 6 We define the *technological imagination* as comprising thinking about answering questions with the possible technological and posing more interesting questions by way of impossible or the highly improbable.

Edinburgh, UK   Phil Turner

Contents

List of Figures

List of Tables

Chapter 1
Imagination

Chapter Thumbnail

Imagination has never received the sustained attention it merits and (consequently) is typically treated as either related to the creation and manipulation of mental imagery or as a synonym for creativity. Yet, as we shall see, neither of these attributions are sufficient to account for all that imagination can do. As Johnson (1987 p. 172) puts it, *"Imagination is central to human meaning and rationality for the simple reason that what we can experience and cognize as meaningful, and how we can reason about it, are both dependent on structures of imagination that make our experience what it is."* In short, imagination, is central to cognition.

In this chapter we consider how imagination has been treated and how it has been defined, how it employs mental simulation and how it is crystallized (i.e. made material). We conclude that despite being one of the most ethereal of psychological faculties, it seems to be primarily oriented towards action and as Brann (1991, p. 6) puts it, imagination "… functions as the interface of world and mind".

1.1 Introduction

> Absolutely everything around us that was created by the hand of man, the entire world of human culture, as distinct from the world of nature, all this is the product of human imagination and of creation based on this imagination
>
> Vygotsky (2004, p. 9)

This book explores the interplay between imagination and digital technology: historically, imagination has proved to be both mysterious and elusive yet despite this, it is claimed to be the source of human culture; in contrast, digital technology is ubiquitous, available, and comprises the very stuff of everyday life for many people. On the surface, these cultural forces could not be more different but on closer examination, surprising synergies are revealed.

© Springer Nature Switzerland AG 2020
P. Turner, *Imagination + Technology*, Human–Computer Interaction Series,
https://doi.org/10.1007/978-3-030-37348-1_1

Imagination is notoriously difficult to define with the philosopher PF Strawson (1970) writing that, "The uses, and applications, of the terms 'image', 'imagine', 'imagination', and so forth make up a very diverse and scattered family. Even this image of a family seems too definite. It would be a matter of more than difficulty to identify and list the family's members, let alone their relations of parenthood and cousinhood". While this is widely acknowledged it has not prevented any number of researchers from attempting definitions, and to risk a sweeping generalisation, these have tended to fall into the "it is the faculty to create and manipulate mental images" variety or are similar to the quotation we began from Vygotsky which treats imagination as "creativity" or the "creative force".

Psychology's position (or lack of it) on imagination is a little difficult to understand particularly as researchers such as Wagoner et al. (2017) claim that "… imagination is involved in every situation in our lives" and if they are right (and it certainly feels that way), imagination should lie at the heart of any account of human cognition but it does not. Perhaps O'Connor and Aardema (2005) are right in suggesting that either the neglect of imagination may be a hangover from Behaviourism or that it is all Freud's fault (more of these points later).

Psychology aside for the moment, our interest here is with the expansive, world-creating form of imagination. We now pose the obvious question which arises: given that imagination is so important ("Absolutely everything …"), why is there no established science or social science of it? There is, of course, no "art" of imagination as art is generally regarded as an inseparable expression of it (e.g. Joy and Sherry 2003). We are not, of course, the first to recognise this, as Lieberman nearly 50 years ago observed, "To some extent, imagination shares with play the dubious distinction that psychologists were reluctant to study it, and the field was left largely to philosophers" (1977/2014 p. 2). Were it that simple, as some philosophers are all too aware of "imagination's tarnished history" and have consequently avoided it (Kaag 2014, p. 9).

Since psychology does not have the body of work we might have hoped for, we must look elsewhere. And the work of Mithen, an anthropologist interested in the origins of mind, offers an interesting place to start. He proposes that imagination is used in support of decision making so, for example, when we inspect a restaurant menu to select a dish from it, he argues that we imagine how the food might taste or which wine to drink with it and so on. In doing so, Mithen claims that when we are imagining such things, we are creating possible future worlds (one where we are vegetarian, one where we select fish and one where we have foresworn drink), and evaluate them (e.g. "the fish dish sounds dull but a nice Chablis might lift it"). So, imagination helps with bounded rationality in a manner resembling the role of affect in decision making (see for example Oatley and Johnson-Laird 1996). He goes on to identify seven pre-conditions required for imagination to develop.

The first three are deemed to be the most important: at the top of the list is the development of a Theory of Mind, which Mithen calls the knowledge that others have beliefs and thoughts that are different from one's own. He suggests that this evolved in response to our distant ancestors being members of larger social groups in which imagination is used for "thought experiments" directed at predicting and making sense of the thoughts and behaviours of others. The second pre-condition is the recognition that we take years and years to mature (if at all). This extended immaturity is a result of being born as helpless babies with large brains and consequently uncomfortably large heads for our slender-hipped mothers. However, being immature allows us to enjoy imaginative play for longer than an equivalent primate. The third pre-condition is the appearance of specialised intelligence in the form of dedicated "mental modules" which can be combined to create new "ideas" (e.g. Mithen 1996, 2006) and this is afforded by way of our imaginations.

In addition to these three pre-conditions come more recent changes to the make-up of our cognition, namely, the development of language which has enabled the creation, sharing and elaboration of ideas and what Mithen calls "cognitive fluidity" and the extended mind hypothesis which involves the use of external representations and technology to store and share ideas (e.g. writing, painting and so forth)—effectively extending our minds beyond the confines of our skulls. Finally, Mithen identifies the rise of the sedentary lifestyle has enabled individuals to spend more time on creative pursuits such as storytelling. Right or wrong, Mithen has successfully illustrated the reach of imagination—from decision making to extended cognition, from language to storytelling and well beyond mere image manipulation.

1.2 Elusive Imagination

The introduction to this chapter has offered a very brief description of some of the problems of working with imagination from a strictly psychological perspective and why, again very briefly, the anthropological approach affords us greater latitude to explore its relationship with digital technology. However, we must return to psychology to address a number of outstanding questions regarding the nature of imagination and the first of these is its relationship with mental imagery.

There seems to be an irresistible urge in many researchers to connect imagination and imagery. Imagination is often associated with the internal "visual" landscape to which we have access, and is often thought of as a kind of "thinking space" filled with mental pictures. Singer and Singer (2007) appear to agree and note that, "Imagination is a form of human thought characterized by the ability of the individual to reproduce images or concepts originally derived from the basic senses, but now reflected in one's consciousness as memories, fantasies, or future plans." (p. 16). In Brann's (1991) *The World of the Imagination*, which has become the standard text, tells us that imagination is "most likely defined straightforwardly as a capacity for seeing things in one's head" (p. 24) which is very much a reiteration of a common observation. Johnson (2013) also tells us that, "imagination is our capacity to organize mental representations (especially percepts, images and image schemata) into meaningful, coherent unities". So, from these perspectives, imagination seems to be a matter of creating and manipulating images and this is reinforced etymologically as both imagination and image naturally suggests something visual. Again, we have Vygotsky (2004) writing that imagination is the ability to "image" or "see" distal or completely constructed worlds and possibilities but he also claims that "every invention, whether large or small, before being implemented, embodied in reality, was held together by the imagination alone" which seems to go beyond simple imagery.

Indeed, any discussion of imagery presents us with its own problems. Imagination-as-image can be tracked back to at least the 17th century with the English philosopher Thomas Hobbes who described imagination as nothing but "decaying sense" (Leviathan, 2). He invites us to consider looking at an object, then removing it. He notes that we retain a diminished image of the thing seen, though more obscure than when we see it. This diminished image, he claims, is called imagination from the image made in seeing. This relationship between imagination and mental imagery is not quite so simple for everyone.

Here we borrow from Kosslyn et al. (2006)'s review, "The case for mental imagery" which they begin by noting that with the demise of Behaviourism, came cognitive psychology (approximately, the mid 1950s) with its enthusiasm for mental representation and hence a new-found interest in mental imagery. Adopting an historical approach, Kosslyn identifies four phases of research into mental imagery/imagination. The first of these was initiated by Pylyshyn in the early 1970s with a focus on the adequacy of different forms of internal representations for imagery. The key question was whether or not the mental images are actually pictorial. The consensus was that all images were actually based on underlying language (explicitly, images are stored as linguistic representations). The second phase which appeared in the early 1980s wondered whether tacit knowledge was being used (unconsciously) by participants in experimental studies to mimic what they thought would occur in perception. Ten years later again, the third phase heralded the use of neuroscientific data to lend a degree of objectivity to experimental studies. With the millennium (taking us to the date of Kosslyn's paper) had come an interest in the relationship between mental phenomena (as a whole) and their underlying neural substrate. At this point, it would be fair to say that Kosslyn has concluded that imagination and imagery are quite different.

Bringing us right up to date, von Stumm and Scott (2019) define imagination as the tendency to create "mental representations of concepts, ideas and sensations in the mind that are not contemporaneously perceived by the senses [and ranges] from the re-creation of images or sensory perceptions in the mind that were previously seen and experienced in reality ... to crafting images anew independent of prior actual sensory input." Clearly, images are an important focus of imagination, though they note that the complexity of their definition is in part, a consequence of what they call the "definition and measurement issues" that have hampered the study of imagination, "including a lack of agreement among psychologists on a precise definition that distinguishes it from related constructs, such as fantasy or mental imagery". Overall, from Kosslyn's review to these contemporary researchers there is little or no reason to suppose that theories of imagery are also theories of imagination.

However, just because we have concluded that imagination and mental imagery are not equivalent does not mean that mental imagery does not play an important role in creative practice such as design, the study of which has been quite diverse. For example, Dahl et al. (1999) have demonstrated that visual mental imagery (by which they mean "the mind's eye") can influence the customer appeal of a product particularly during the design phase; while Oxman (2002) has examined the externalization of design thinking in drawing and sketching from the perspective of mental imagery and Yoo and Kim (2014) have sought to stimulate the creation of mental imagery (which they claim stimulates positive emotion) in what we assume to be potential consumers when presenting products online.

With the imagination/imagery issue addressed at least for the moment we can now move to consider how imagination has been treated with regard to providing a source of integration or "narrative glue"; then as the means by which we plan and strategy-test; and then imagination and counter-factional thinking; and affect, reflecting that imagination often acts as a multi-purpose "Swiss Army knife".

Imagination and "filling in the gaps"
There have been a number of writers from both philosophy and psychology who attribute the power of *integration* to imagination. Dewey (1934, p. 267), for example, wrote that, "The imagination is a way of seeing and feeling things as they compose an integral whole. It is the large and general blending of interest at the point where the mind comes in contact with the world. When old and familiar things are made new in experience there is imagination".

Similarly, Thomas (no date) writing from a psychological perspective suggests that, "Imagination is what makes our sensory experience meaningful, enabling us to interpret and make sense of it, whether from a conventional perspective or from a fresh, original, individual one. It is what makes perception more than the mere physical stimulation of sense organs. It also produces mental imagery, visual and otherwise, which is what makes it possible for us to think outside the confines of our present perceptual reality, to consider memories of the past and possibilities for the future, and to weigh alternatives against one another. Thus, imagination makes possible all our thinking about what is, what has been, and, perhaps most important, what might be."

In a related vein, Pelaprat and Cole (2011) have proposed that imagination is a "gap-filling" process, writing that, "imagination is the process of resolving and connecting the fragmented, poorly coordinated experience of the world so as to bring about a stable image of the world [...]. The fragmented nature of human experience ineluctably exists, we argue, from the fact that the human mind is simultaneously constrained by phylogeny, cultural history, and ontogenesis all operating on their own time scales and in accordance with differing mechanisms of change. We therefore characterize imagination as a "gap-filling" process".

And, Hobbes as noted by Debus (2014) claims that "imagination and memory are but one thing, which for diverse reasons, have diverse names". She notes that this surprising equivalence is based on the observation that both enable us to think about things which are not or are no long present. Fesmire (2003) also identifies two roles of imagination, firstly, imagination as "empathic projection," as a way to respond directly and empathically to others and their feelings and thoughts; and secondly, imagination as a way to escape current patterns and imagine alternatives, concluding that imagination is "*a capacity to engage the present with an eye to what is not immediately at hand.*"

Imagination and strategy testing

On an everyday basis, we treat imagination as a means of generating ideas, tackling problems, dealing with a difficult situation ("just use your imagination"), or even spending a windfall, and most importantly, all without committing ourselves to any specific course of action. Thus, we can plan and evaluate the possible and probable without threat or danger to ourselves. This is imagination as "what-if" thinking.

Unlike much of the psychological research in the West, there is a psychological approach which has a place for imagination particularly in this form, and it will come as no surprise that Lev Vygotsky was behind it. This school of thought is more fully described as cultural-historical activity theory or Activity Theory for short, which immediately distinguishes itself from Western psychological thinking. Activity theorists use the term "inner plane of action" or IPA which, in the developing child, provides for a new form of interaction between internal and external activities. The argument runs like this, initially, a child only has control over things in the external world by way of simple action and feedback loops. However, cognitive development for the child involves the successive internalisation of such activities, thus the child acquires the ability to perform or *rehearse* some of these activities in their "mind's eye"—or IPA, before committing to action. This, of course, offers significant advantages over committing to a plan in the real world with all the unfortunate consequences that might have. We note that one of the key attractions of digital technology is that it frequently embodies this ability to explore the what-if, in for example, the what-if analysis functions in spreadsheets or the preview facilities in document processing.

Currie has also proposed that both imagination and pretence can serve to "test-run" possible courses of action which he calls "strategy testing" or simulation (Currie 1995, p. 158). In short, strategy testing is using imagination to simulate a scenario. He describes these simulation as follows: "Running a test in the simulator should be a bit like having the experiences we would have if we really were acting out the strategy. Not quite like it, of course. That would be difficult, and dangerous too, because it would amount to the conditions of an hallucination. A compromise would be to reproduce the kinds of affective states we would have if the test were real. In the real case affective states are mediated by our beliefs and desires; we feel the sensations of fear not because the tiger is about to attack us but because we believe it is and desire it not to. So, what the simulator does is to retain the connections between inner representation and bodily sensation that would be there if the representation was functioning as a belief; what is not retained is the belief-like connection to behaviour." (1995, p. 157).

Imagination and counterfactual thinking

Without wishing to pre-empt our discussion of fiction (beginning Sect. 2.4), we can at least say that we can imagine worlds that do not but might have existed and reason about what might go on in them. In her *The Rational Imagination*, Byrne (2005) is more specific and claims that imagination allows us to create counterfactual alternatives to reality and by way of example, she opens her account by wondering about Martin Luther King Jr.'s assassination in 1968 while he was only thirty-nine years old, and asks "who can say what would have happened if he had lived longer? (p. 1).[1]

So, this is reasoning about a fictional world is a common enough device used by novelists. For example, both Robert Harris's *Fatherland* and Len Deyton's *SS GB* were set in a Europe dominated by a triumphant Nazi party. These novels work, not least because they are brilliantly written but because they are plausible. In these novels people still go to work, get tired, angry, or are happy. Walton (1990), observes that games, cinema, and a variety of other media are governed by "principles of generation" which are "reality-oriented". The reality in question is, of course, based on similarities to the real world (of the "going to work", "getting tired" variety). He also proposes the mutual belief principle for fantastic worlds, based on a tacit agreement between the creator of these worlds and those who experience them, (e.g. all aliens species speak idiomatic American English; and that inter-stellar flight is not only plausible but is widespread).

Imagination and affect

And then there is the matter of imagination and affect. As Taylor (1999, p. 6) observes, "one of the special functions of pretend play is to help children control and master their emotions". A view which is supported by the work on *imaginary friends* which suggests that these invisible companions serve a variety of emotional needs, not least the desire for companionship, but also provide a way to work through fears or a method of dealing with actual or perceived restriction". It has been estimated that approximately half of all children have imaginary friends, and these friends often act as companions or playmates for many years. For example, the crime novelist Agatha Christie, for example, is reported to have had a lifelong relationship with hers while the musician Kurt Cobain did address his suicide note to his imaginary companion, Boddah.

Unsurprisingly, the relationship between imagination and affect has received a measure of experimental investigation, for example, small children are afraid of monsters which Harris (2000), describes as genuine, rather than being an excuse to avoiding going to bed early, and these genuine fears can interfere with everyday life. For example, Harris cites the work of Newson and Newson (1968) who describe a

---

[1]The economist magazine (https://www.economist.com/the-world-if/2018/07/05/a-different-dream) speculated on this and offered this warning, *"Though it is often a mistake to attribute too much power to shape history to a single person, King's death was the spur for improvements in civil rights and race relations that might not otherwise have occurred. Had he made it through 1968 alive, however, he would have ended the 1960 s as a controversial, divisive figure for many white Americans. A Gallup poll in 1966 found that only 32% of Americans had a positive view of King. In a Gallup survey in 1967 to identify the ten most-admired Americans, George Wallace, the segregationist governor of Alabama, made the list. King did not".*
The National Geographic magazine published their own thought experiment on this too (https://www.nationalgeographic.co.uk/history-and-civilisation/2018/04/what-if-martin-luther-king-jr-were-never-assassinated) and speculated whether "Dr. King may have successfully run for president as Mandela did."

child who was so afraid of the imaginary monkeys which lived in their cellar, that he never went down there because of them.

Gendler (2008) has proposed a new form of believe—the alief which is "*a*ssociative, *a*ction-generating, *a*ffect-laden, *a*rational, *a*utomatic, *a*gnostic with respect to its content, shared with animals, and developmentally and conceptually antecedent to other cognitive attitudes" (the leading italicised a's are hers). An alief is also defined as an habitual propensity to respond automatically and affective to particular stimuli. So, for example, Gendler also tells us that while a subject may believe that drinking out of a sterile bedpan is completely safe, she may nonetheless show hesitation and disgust at the prospect of doing so because the bedpan invokes an alief with the content "filthy object, disgusting, stay away". By way of further example, Gendler describes the effect produced by walking on the glass-floored Grand Canyon Skywalk as an alief incorporating "the visual appearance as of a cliff, the feeling of fear and the motor routine of retreat".

A cognitive "Swiss army knife"?
Like those before us, we recognise that the thinking on imagination is both broad and diverse but also rather "siloed". There is imagination and make-believe from a developmental perspective; imaginative thinking from the perspective of fiction; make-believe and aesthetic appreciation; imagination as counter-factional thinking or as strategy-testing; imagination as mental image creation and manipulation. And this is without considering the anthropological, or the neurological or the social. In all, it is treated differently by different researchers and commentators. But perhaps more than that it has a note of general purpose or better, multi-purpose about it—a little like a Swiss army knife.

I use my own Swiss army knife for opening cardboard boxes, cutting string on parcels, pulling corks from bottles of wine and quite often as a screwdriver and there seems to be a parallel between it and what Wagoner (2017) and his colleagues have observed about imagination. "Imagination is not seen here as an isolated cognitive faculty but as how people anticipate and constructively move towards an indeterminate future".

1.3   The Material Basis of Imagination

A key question must be, where does imagination come from? In one sense, the answer is quite simple, it comes from a rehash of prior experience. Vygotsky puts this more elegantly: "everything the imagination creates is based on elements taken from reality, from a person's previous experience", so our personal past, our histories provide from the material basis of our imagination.

Vygotsky proposes that imagination is governed by four "laws" the first of which is that the creative activity of the imagination depends directly on the richness and variety of a person's previous experience because this experience provides the material from which the product so fantasy is constructed. The richer a person's experience, the richer the material his imagination has access to. Following this means, to the chagrin of all proud parents, children cannot be particularly imaginative because they simply haven't been alive long enough to have very many experiences—even the very indulged ones.

The second law introduces a social factor or a sense of indirection. It is noteworthy that Vygotsky remains the only theorist to have introduced an explicit social dimension. So, let us imagine a famous event, say the Battle of Hastings. This is, of course, governed by Vygotsky's first law—the detail is a matter of our knowledge and experience of early Middle Ages armed conflict, but as we were not present in southern England in 1066 when William landed, what we know of it is based on the experience of others and the Bayeux tapestry is an excellent example of this. The tapestry is filled with representations of the Norman invader and the English defenders and iconic image of Harold, the English king with a foreign arrow in his eye. Add to this the TV programmes about the Norman conquest of England and how the English language has changed (e.g. the French motto "*honi soit qui mal y pense*" still appears in the British passport). But there is and could be no first-hand experience of the events.

Vygostky's third law concerns imagination and affect. He writes that, "Emotions thus possess a kind of capacity to select impressions, thoughts, and images that resonate with the mood that possesses us at a particular moment in time. Everyone knows that we see everything with completely different eyes depending on whether we are experiencing at the same time grief or joy". He further suggests that colour provides an internal language for our emotion, for example, sorrow and mourning are indicated by the colour black.

The fourth and final law relates to the association between imagination and reality is that a construct of "fantasy" may represent something substantially new, never encountered before in human experience and without correspondence to any object that actually exists in reality; however, once it has been externally embodied, that is, has been given material form, this crystallized imagination that has become an object begins to actually exist in the real world, to affect other things. In this way imagination becomes reality and examples of such crystallized or embodied imagination include any technical device, machine, or instrument.

1.4 Mental Simulation and Imagination

The last twenty years have seen a growing body of evidence that a wide range of experiences and behaviours share many common neural structures. These experiences include everyday action such as walking and talking in the real world, but more importantly for the current discussion, imagining walking and talking, dreaming about walking and talking and even watching (and understanding and anticipating) other people walking and talking. This suggests that imagination may draw upon our ability to create *mental simulations*.

It makes better sense that those parts of the brain responsible for, say, actions involved in walking across a room are also used when we imagine walking across a room too (but without engaging "execute"). The same is true for (night-time) dreams which involve walking about: again, it is reasonable to suppose that the day-time neural structures and pathways is appropriated by the "nightshift". Indeed, it makes less sense to suppose the notion that there is another discrete set of neural structures enabling us to reproduce waking activity when we are dreaming. Having accepted these proposals as plausible, it is a relatively short step to recruit these neural pathways to re-creating or, in a sense re-enacting, scenes from a book we might be reading. And indeed, it is the case that a number of accounts of reading comprehension implicate the same regions of the brain involved in equivalent perceptions and actions in the real world (Barsalou 1999; Glenberg 1997). These theories argue that the same representations used for making or watching a real-world activity are involved when someone reads about that activity. Further, there is fMRI evidence that as people read stories which involve tracking characters' movements and motivations the same areas of the brain are active as when "people perform, imagine, or observe similar real-world activities" (Speer et al. 2009).

Jeannerod (2001) has proposed that we create an internal simulation (more often described as "motor imagery") of the actions we are about to take before we actually execute them, and this simulation is usually produced without unconscious thought. So, for example, I am about to take a break from typing to reach for my coffee cup, but while the intention is conscious, the simulation underpinning the execution is not. At no point do I consciously calculate the angle my elbow needs to move from and to; nor do I work out how my fingers and thumb open and close around the cup, the upward movement of my right forearm and so on. As for the complexity of sipping the hot coffee … Simulating these actions in advance of their execution, Jeannerod and his colleagues argue, minimises errors and offers the many benefits of practice. This begs the question of how are these simulations related to the actual motor action? Here, Decety's methods for comparing real and simulated tasks have proved to be highly revealing. His measurements include mental chronometry, monitoring autonomic responses and measuring cerebral blood flow in people performing both real and simulated, imaginary tasks, for example, when Decety et al. (1996) asked people to imagine "walking" toward points placed at different distances, they found that the time it took to perform this task varied according to the actual distance of the target. Then repeating this task in the real world, they also found that the times were also highly correlated with the task carried out in the imagination. In a second round of experiments, they asked people to imagine themselves walking toward a target while carrying different loads. Again, it was found that people took longer to reach the target carrying a heavy load as compared to imagining themselves to be unburdened (Decety 1996). Taken together, these findings suggest that motor imagery and motor production exploit the same representations and that the physical characteristics of objects and events exert an influence on both imagined and performed actions. Indeed, Sirigu and her colleagues (1996) have shown that imagined actions follow the same speed-accuracy trade-offs as embodied in Fitts' Law.

Table 1.1 Adapted from Jeannerod (2001) (Table 2, p. S104)

Brain regions and Brodmann areas (Ba) engaged	Execute	Imagine	Observe actions
Precentral gyrus Ba 4	✓	✓	✓
Precentral gyrus (dorsal) Ba 6	✓	✓	✓
Precentral gyrus (ventral) Ba 6	✓	✓	✓
Supplementary Motor Area (rostral) Ba 6	✓	✓	✓
Cingular gyrus Ba 24	✓	✓	

Decety went on to propose that motor images, that is, self-created mental images of skilled motor actions—such as skiing, playing cricket, drinking coffee, share the same neural mechanisms as those that are also responsible for preparation and programming of actual movements. His argument, in essence, is that motor acts are represented centrally and as such are available for modification, retrieval and execution. Motor imagery and motor *execution* differ only in that the former is blocked at some level of the cortico-spinal flow.[2]

These initial ideas and findings were subsequently developed by Jeannerod (2001) to create his "theory of neural simulation of action" which states that real and imagined actions are mediated by the same cortical areas. Jeannerod's hypothesis is that the motor system is part of a simulation network that is activated when we intend acting or when we have observed others engaged in an activity or other. He argues that the function of this simulation not only shapes the motor system in anticipation of execution, but also to provide information as to both the feasibility and the meaning of potential actions. Table 1.1, which has been adapted from Jeannerod (ibid), is a simplified summary of 14 reported studies which support his account.

Erlacher and Schredl (2008) have extended this discussion by examining the hypothesis that REM dreams also call upon these same neural substrates. Their approach has been to review the literature on dreams against the Jeannerod/Decety position. They found abundant anecdotal evidence from studies of the reported dreams of athletes—who have reported "practicing" difficult or demanding procedures in lucid dreams—and clinical evidence from people suffering from REM sleep behaviour disorder and invasive animal studies. In all, the strongest support for the shared substrate hypothesis was from the central nervous activity (recorded) during REM sleep.

Emulation

The emulation theory of representation (Grush 2004) is a framework that claims to synthesize a variety of representational functions of the brain based on reasoning, control theory and signal processing algorithms. In brief, Grush argues that the brain constructs representations of the body and environment, then during overt

---

[2]Jeannerod (2001) notes that basal ganglia are activated during imagined actions and that execution and imagination engage different parts of the striatum. The putamen, which is part of a purely sensorimotor corticocortical loop, is activated during execution, while the head of the caudate (part of the cognitive loop) is active during imagination.

sensorimotor engagement these models not only simulate behavior but also provide expectations of the sensory feedback. So, Grush means that not only do we create motor programs to, say pick up a cup of coffee, but also, we create the imagined sensory responses to picking up that cup—how the cup feels to the hand, the heat of the coffee, the expected weight of the cup and so forth. These models can also be run "off-line" (that is, without the intention to execute the motor programs) in order to produce mental imagery, estimate outcomes of different actions, and evaluate and develop motor plans.

Grush argues that the simulation theory is only "half correct", namely the efferent motor programme aspects which he adopts as the first half of his emulation account. The problem, then, with simulation theory per se is it is conceived of against the backdrop of closed-loop control, and motor imagery which is hypothesized to be the "free-spinning of the controller" (motor centres) when disengaged from the body. In contrast, emulation theory, imagery is not produced by the mere "free-spinning" operation of the efferent motor areas, but by these areas themselves driving an emulator of the musculoskeletal system. Grush argues that there are reasons for preferring the emulation theory over simulation theory hinge on the observation that the operation of the motor centres, in themselves, is insufficient for motor imagery. Grush offers an analogy to underline the difference between his emulation theory and simulation theory. He writes, "motor imagery is like a pilot sitting in a flight simulator, and the pilot's efferent commands (hand and foot movements, etc.) are translated into faux "sensory" information (instrument readings, mock visual display) by the flight simulator which is essentially an emulator of an aircraft. The simulation theory claims that just a pilot, moving her hands and feet around but driving neither a real aircraft nor a flight simulator, is sufficient for mock sensory information", p. 380.

Sitting between these two models and from a philosophical perspective Van Leeuwen has proposed his *Active Imagination Thesis* which is based on a form of imagining that comprises a continuously updated "forward model of action in the world". This forward model itself comprises the possible actions which might be taken selected from the available perceptual representations. These might be veridical, non-veridical, or in some mixture. The "non-veridical" perceptual representations are imaginary. This model is of interest as it proposes a way of integrating the imaginary into the real-world perceptual field. Example of this are readily available in make-believe (pretend) play or in acting on the stage.

Mirroring and quarantining

Games of pretence in particular, and imaginative episodes in general, tend to share a pair of features that have been dubbed mirroring and quarantining (Gendler 2003; see also Leslie 1987; Perner 1991; Nichols and Stich 2000).

Mirroring is manifest to the extent that features of the imaginary situation that have not been explicitly stipulated are derivable via features of their real-world analogues, or, more generally, to the extent that imaginative content is taken to be governed by the same sorts of restrictions that govern believed content. For example, in a widely-discussed experiment conducted by Leslie (1994), children are asked to engage in an imaginary tea party. When an experimenter tips and 'spills' one of the (empty) teacups, children consider the non-tipped cup to be 'full' (in the context of the pretence) and the tipped cup to be 'empty' (both within and outside of the context of the pretence). More generally, it appears that both games of make-believe and more complicated engagements with fiction, cinema, and visual art are governed by principles of generation, according to which particular prompts or props 'generate' or 'render make-believe' particular fictional truths and that those principles tend to be, for the most part, reality-oriented.

Quarantining is manifest to the extent that events within the imagined or pretended episode are taken to have effects only within a relevantly circumscribed domain. So, for example, a child engaging in the make-believe tea party does not expect that 'spilling' (imaginary) 'tea' will result in the table really being wet, nor does a person who imagines winning the lottery expect that when she visits the ATM, her bank account will contain riches. More generally, quarantining is manifest to the extent that proto-beliefs and proto-attitudes concerning the imagined state of affairs are not treated as beliefs and attitudes relevant to guiding action in the actual world. The failure to quarantine imaginary attitudes in certain contexts is often taken to be a mark of mental illness). Some (Nichols and Stich 2000, 2003; cf. Leslie 1987) have suggest that mirroring and quarantining fall out naturally from the architecture of the imagination: mirroring is a consequence of the ways in which imagination and belief share a "single code" and quarantining is a consequence of the way in which imagination takes place "off-line" (Nichols 2004, 2006).

Though pretence and imaginative are governed by these two principles, both may be violated in systematic ways. Mirroring gives way to disparity as a result of the ways in which (the treatment of) imaginary content may differ from (that of) believed content. Imagined content may be incomplete (e.g. there may be no fact of the matter (in the pretence) just how much tea has spilled on the table) or incoherent (e.g. it might be that the toaster serves (in the pretence) as a logical-truth inverter). And content that is imagined may give rise to discrepant responses, most strikingly in cases of discrepant affect (where, for example, the imminent destruction of all human life is treated as amusing rather than terrifying; cf. Nichols 2006, also Gendler 2003, 2006)

Quarantining gives way to contagion when imagined content ends up playing a direct role in actual attitudes and behaviour. This is common in cases of affective transmission, where an emotional response generated by an imagined situation may constrain subsequent behaviour. For example, imagining something fearful (such as a tiger in the kitchen) may give rise to actual hesitation (such as reluctance to enter the room; cf. Harris 2000.) And this, of course, recalls Slater's experiments with the virtual reality recreation of the famous visual cliff experiment (1994) and offers an alternative explanation of his findings. In these experiments, participants were found to hesitate when faced with a virtual "pit". The relevance of contagion to presence research may also some way in explaining the successful use of virtual reality in the treatment of phobias (e.g. Rothbaum et al. 1995, 1996; Botella et al. 1998; Emmelkamp et al. 2002). In these instances, virtual (imaginary) spiders, flying, confined spaces and so forth have been used to systematically de-sensitise those suffering from the corresponding phobias by presenting them with the object of their fear in a safe, managed environment but one which is capable of evoking an affective response. Perhaps, even more dramatically, Hoffman et al. (2011) have reported the successful use of virtual reality technology in the pain management of burns treatment. In their study, they reported that the feeling of cold (induced by a snowy landscape) can be used to reduce the pain from real world burns suffered by servicemen.

It also occurs in cases of cognitive transmission, where imagined content is thereby "primed" and rendered more accessible in ways that go on to shape subsequent perception and experience. For example, imagining some object (such as a sheep) may make one more likely to "perceive" proximal objects in one's environment (such as mistaking a figure for an amorous ram).

1.5   Metaphor and Imagination

We propose here that we imagine because we care, not just because we can, and we distinguish between imaginative content and the imaginative process.

Evidence suggests that the content of an imaginative episode appears to comprise a collage of fragments of things we have experienced drawn from semantic, episodic and autobiographical memory (e.g. Vygotsky 1931/2004; Tulving 2002a, b; Hassabis and Maguire 2007; Schacter et al. 2007, 2012, 2013). So, the content of imagination is primarily a rehash or re-ordering or re-presentation of experiences but how does this work?

We propose this is achieved by assigning one thing to stand for another thing which involves, for example, shifting perspective from the here-and-now to a possible future; or to what I imagine is your point of view; or seeing a mobile phone as a mental health "buddy"; or to that of the narrator in an adventure story. This process of assignment or substitution is what is meant by metaphor (etymologically, metaphor means transference). We shall more usually refer to this as *seeing-as*. As these four metaphors are the subject of Chap. 2 we will only develop these ideas a little so as to give a flavour of what is to come.

Imagination enables us to make-sense of the world by way of something else (metaphor). This proposal, of course, runs the risk of turning all of us into three-year olds endlessly asking "why?". If we can only understand A with reference to B and B with reference to C, just where is the end (or starting) point? We need to identify a point from which all such explanations (or metaphors) flow.

While Fodor (1998), argues that this starting point is our innate repertoire of concepts, Lakoff and Johnson (1999) argue more compellingly that the real source lies with our corporeality. So, this is to say that the way we understand complex stuff is by building on simpler stuff and at the end of the chain, are the sensorimotor experiences we have had for as long as we have had senses and motor functions—in short, have had bodies. And by experiences we include conceptualising, reasoning about, visualising and imagining.

The importance of our embodiment to the workings of our cognition (and hence the term, "embodied cognition") has been successively constructed from the work of thinkers and researchers over the last 60 years or so. These include (please note that this is more of a "name check") the French philosopher Merleau-Ponty who probably can take credit for starting this off, then successively Varela, Thompson and Rosch's *The Embodied Mind* (1991); *Clark's Being There* (1997) and Dourish's (2001) *Where the action is*. We should also mention Sheets-Johnstone who tells us that she instigated the "corporeal turn" in the 1980s in response to what she describes as 350 years of Cartesian misrepresentation. She writes of the body as the "material handmaiden of an all-powerful mind, a necessary but ultimately discountable aspect of cognition, intelligence and affectivity" (Sheets-Johnstone 2009, p. 2).

These different writers have presented their own perspective on embodiment/corporeality but it is the work of Lakoff and Johnson and their *Philosophy of the Flesh* which is most relevant to the current discussion on imagination (Lakoff and Johnson 1999). Writing of the mind they observe that it is inherently embodied; and that thought is mostly unconscious; and, most importantly, that abstract concepts are largely metaphorical. They describe how we use bodily "projections" to orientate ourselves in space, for example, the projections "in front of" and "to the right of" are, of course to be understood in terms of having a body as we have inherent fronts and backs. We see from the front, normally move in the direction our fronts are oriented, and interact with objects and other people at our fronts. We also project fronts and backs onto objects (ibid, p. 34). These projections, in turn, are a consequence of the corresponding sensorimotor experiences of something being in front of us – and so on. They go on to tell us that with continued exposure to the world, these embodied experiences become conceptualised as metaphors and it is these embodied metaphors which underpin our conceptual knowledge of the world of thought itself. Our experiences of the world are not, of course, limited to spatial relationships but also afford direct experience of such concepts as FULL-EMPTY and BIG-SMALL and it is the knowledge of these and other relationships which enables us to make sense of the world. We can extend this to encompass the whole world with reference to another real or imaginary world (e.g. *Utopia planitia*, or say "socialist paradise").

Since their philosophical work, evidence has emerged from fMRI studies which tends to support their position. For example, on hearing a metaphor such as "she had a rough day," those parts of the brain responsible for tactile experience become activated. Similarly, learning that someone is "sweet" activates those areas responsible for gustation, and more particularly, an invitation to act (used metaphorically) like "grasping a concept" or "bending the rules" involves those centres implicated in motor perception and planning (Lai and Curran 2013). In subsequent work Lai and her colleagues (Lai et al. 2019) using EEG to record electrical activity in the brain, have further confirmed this earlier evidence. Experimental participants were shown three different sentences: one described a concrete action, such as, "The bodyguard bent the rod"; another was the metaphorical form of the same verb, for example, "The church bent the rules" and in the third instance, the verb was replaced with a more abstract word that conveyed the same meaning, for example, "The church altered the rules." The results showed that when participants saw the word "bent" used in both the literal and metaphorical context, the sensorimotor region the brain being activated almost immediately. The third form did not show the same response.

Lai concluded that the very rapid activation of the sensorimotor region of the brain suggested that it was important in comprehension of the verbs.

1.6 Defining Imagination

Taking a lead from Mithen's proposal, we propose that imagination is something other than a traditionally conceived cognitive faculty. Indeed, the very act of treating imagination as though it were narrowly cognitive (the "information processing" and "symbol-manipulation" treatments) may have contributed to the difficulty that people have had in defining it.

Putting imagination in a "box"

We have already noted that imagination is not a popular research topic with academics, but we have not suggested why this should be so. O'Connor and Aardema (2005, p. 234), who we cited earlier, have identified three different factors.

Firstly, they observe that the "linguistic turn" in philosophy may have had an effect. This "turn" shifted the focus of philosophical thought and research to the relationship between language and thought and away from phenomena like imagination (e.g. Rorty 1967). Similarly, the dominant paradigm in psychology for the first half of the twentieth century was Behaviourism. The obstacle Behaviourism presented to those interested in imagination was that it had no place for "mental images". As the founding father of Behaviourism, John Watson was to observe, "What does a person mean when he closes his eyes or ears (figuratively speaking) and says, "I see the house where I was born, the trundle bed in my mother's room where I used to sleep—I can even see my mother as she comes to tuck me in and I can even hear her voice as she softly says good night"? He continues, "The behaviourist finds no proof of imagery in all of this. We have put all these things in words, long, long ago". (Watson 1928, pp. 76–77). Then, nearly 50 years later, perhaps the most celebrated of all Behaviourists, Skinner himself wrote just as firmly, that "There are no 'iconic representations' in his mind; there are no "data structures stored in his memory"; he has no "cognitive map" of the world in which he has lived" (Skinner 1974, p. 82–84). Even with the post-war decline of Behaviourism and the advent of cognitivism, no place was to be found for imagination. O'Connor and Aardema conclude by noting that even Freud may have contributed to the demise of interest in imagination by linking it with what they describe as the "uncomfortable" topics of hallucination and fantasy.

Another problem for imagination is that it is not a typical psychological phenomenon. Again, we are not the first to suggest this as Descartes in his Mediations (first published 1641) wrote, " ... this power of imagination which is in one, inasmuch as it differs from the power of understanding, is in no wise a necessary element in my nature, or in the essence of my mind; for although I did not possess it I should doubtless ever remain the same as I now am, from which it appears that we might conclude that it depends on something which differs from me." In short, Descartes neither believes that he possesses imagination (it is not part of his mind) nor it is a part of the essential Descartes. If this is so, it may be worth taking a moment to contrast imagination with other psychological faculties which have also presented difficulties in their definition but nonetheless are still recognisable as distinct domains of study. It is a matter of academic record that there is limited agreement on just how many forms of memory there are and whether the epistemological, neurological and cognitive treatments of memory can ever be reconciled. Despite this, we can mostly agree that we are still discussing memory. Indeed, undergraduate textbooks are filled with diagrams illustrating the operation of memory (or cognition or affect or some such). These often take the form of labelled boxes with arrows connecting them together into flowing sequences of information (or nerve impulses) from processor to buffer, often with a feedback loop, until some psychological state is achieved—a word is recalled, a face is recognised, or a limb is raised. Alternatively, these diagrams may be more "architectural" and comprise block diagrams of a proposed structure of what is being discussed. In such figures we can see, for example, that system A and system B are separate, comprise different elements and operate in parallel. We have raised this issue of diagrammatic representation because there are no such diagrams of imagination. Of course, we have not (could not) have checked every edition of every textbook or monograph, but the point is readily taken. Nowhere is imagination treated "architecturally" like memory or cognition, nor is it envisaged as a sequence of information processing. No one has put imagination in a box.

These absences are curious as most researchers would continue to regard imagination as being a meaningful psychological faculty, like memory and if not, they might struggle to say otherwise. Perhaps this is the reluctance of which Lieberman spoke earlier in this chapter or an unwanted legacy of Behaviourism but there are a growing number of reports of artificial intelligence systems being gifted with imagination so the subject can hardly be regarded as being of no interest to the wider community (Weber et al. 2017; Racanière et al. 2017).

A three-part definition of imagination
Our definition of imagination is in three parts. Firstly, we propose that imagination is how we

i. Engage and make-sense of the world but this is primarily directed at the world of the possible. We all, every day and everywhere, want to anticipate what might happen or what we can expect to happen or ought to happen or should happen or might happen. The very richness of the available vocabulary (e.g. should, ought, might) is telling of our interest in this. The ever prolific Vygotsky (1930/2004, p. 9) tells us that, "the human being [is] a creature oriented toward the future, creating the future and thus altering his own present". He is not alone in this observation and we recognise that we are all "future-prone" and this connection to the future maybe what Merleau-Ponty describes as the intentional arc: "The life of consciousness—cognitive life, the life of desire or perceptual life—is subtended by an 'intentional arc' which projects round about us our past, our future, our human setting, our physical, ideological and moral situation" (Merleau-Ponty 1962: p. 136). The imagination operates as though it were extending before us and actively examines, proposes and considers who or what is coming towards us, whether this is physically, temporarily, existentially. This "intentional arc" is the knowledge of how to act in a way that 'coheres' with one's environment bringing body and world together. But this is more than just being physically present in the world, for example, the intentional arc can be seen in action with the maximal or maximum grip. According to Merleau-Ponty, higher animals and human beings are always trying to get a maximal grip on their situation. When we are looking at something, we tend, without thinking about it, to find the best distance for taking in both the thing and its different parts. When grasping something, we tend to grab it in such a way as to get the best grip on it. Further, Merleau-Ponty has proposed that an intentional arc binds the body to the world, so for example, the movement of the lived body creates (produces) existential space, not the 'objective' movement of the body as such, but it is the experience of this movement. He writes, "Far from my body's being for me no more than a fragment of space, there would be no space at all for me if I had no body". To feel our body feeling its surroundings is not merely an exercise in self-reflection but how we 'prehend' the world (ibid). This kinaesthetic feedback is how we both objectify the world and orient ourselves within it. Thus, imagination may be a manifestation of an "intentional arc" and we propose that we imagine because we are engaged with the world. This is also to recognise that imagination is geared towards the action and the practical.

ii. Predicting or anticipating the future is not an intellectual (or worse, a mere academic exercise as it matters to us) and since psychology cannot easily tell us why we care (are concerned), so like so many before us, we must turn to philosophy and the work of Heidegger (1927/1962). Heidegger prefers the term Dasein when writing about human beings, and observes that Dasein is in the world. This is the central fact of our being and is more fundamental than whether we are thinking or not (cf. Descartes' cogito ergo sum). Not only are we, in-the-world but we are in a world that matters to us. A consequence to being-in-the-world is that we are involved with it, and this is not optional. We are involved with the world whether we like it or not and we cannot escape it (except through powerful drugs or a blow to the head). Another way of say "being in the world" for Heidegger is to say that we are with others, which is social recasting of this insight (that is, we are with others in an artefactual world). As for care specifically, Heidegger writes that it is expressed as projection, thrownness and fallness (the oddity of vocabulary is typical of Heidegger). Of these expressions, projection is probably the most relevant here as it refers to our orientation towards the future and the realm of its possibilities. Heidegger writes that all human beings are "ahead of themselves" which can be translated as "to anticipate" or being on "the lookout for what to do" and this looking ahead is what imagination is about. So, following Heidegger, we are in the world, we care about it and are consequently involved with it, and imagination is our way of making sense of this.

iii. Finally, if we are to make sense of the possible and what might be going through the mind of another we need to be able to shift perspective and to access stories which tell us who we are and embody culture. And all of these fundamentally are based on the creation and manipulation of metaphor which are themselves are the bases of cognition.

References

Barsalou LW (1999) Perceptual symbol systems. Behav Brain Sci 22(4):577–660

Botella C, Baños RM, Perpiñá C, Villa H, Alcañiz M, Rey A (1998) Virtual reality treatment of claustrophobia: a case report. Behav Res Ther 36(2):239–246

Brann ET (1991) The world of the imagination: sum and substance. Rowman & Littlefield Publishers, Lanham, Maryland

Byrne R (2005) The Rational Imagination: how people create alternatives to reality. MIT Press, Cambridge, MA

Currie G (1995) Imagination as simulation: aesthetics meets cognitive science. In: Davies M, Stone T (eds) Mental simulation: evaluations and applications. Blackwell, Oxford

Dahl D, Chattopadhyay A, Gorn G (1999) The use of visual mental imagery in new product design. J Mark Res 36:18. https://doi.org/10.2307/3151912

Debus D (2014) 'Mental time travel': remembering the past, imagining the future, and the particularity of events. Rev Philos Psychol 5(3):333–350. https://doi.org/10.1007/s13164-014-0182-7

Decety J (1996) Do imagined and executed actions share the same neural substrate? Cogn Brain Res 3:87–93

Decety J (1996) Do imagined and executed actions share the same neural substrate? Cogn Brain Res 3(2)87–93

Dewey J (1934) Art as experience. Minton, Balch & Co, New York

Emmelkamp PMG, Krijn M, Hulsbosch L, de Vries S, Schuemie MJ, van der Mast CAPG (2002) Virtual reality treatment versus exposure in vivo: a comparative evaluation in acrophobia. Behav Res Ther 40:25–32

Erlacher D, Schredl M (2008) Do REM (lucid) dreamed and executed actions share the same neural substrate? Int J Dream Res pp 7–14

Fesmire S (2003) John dewey and moral imagination: pragmatism in Ethics. Indiana University Press, Bloomington, IN

Fodor JA (1998) Concepts: where cognitive science went wrong. Oxford University Press, New York

Gendler TS (2003) On the relation between pretence and belief. In: Kieran and Lopes, pp 125–41

Gendler TS (2006) Imaginative resistance revisited. Nichols 2006:149–173

Gendler TS (2008) Alief and belief. J Philos 105(10)

Glenberg AM (1997) What memory is for. Behav Brain Sci 20:1–19

Grush R (2004) The emulation theory of representation: motor control, imagery, and perception. Behav Brain Sci 27:377–442

Harris PL (2000) The work of the imagination. Blackwell Publishing, Oxford

Hassabis D, Maguire EA (2007) Deconstructing episodic memory with construction. Trends Cogn Sci 11(7):299–306

Heidegger M (1927/1962) Being and Time (trans: Macquarrie J, Robinson E) New York: Harper Collins

Hoffman HG, Chambers GT, Meyer III WJ, Arceneaux LL, Russell WJ, Seibel EJ, ... Patterson DR (2011) Virtual reality as an adjunctive non-pharmacologic analgesic for acute burn pain during medical procedures. Ann Behav Med 41(2):183–191

Jeannerod M (2001) Neural simulation of action: a unifying mechanism for motor cognition. NeuroImage 14:S103–S109

Johnson M (1987) The body in the mind: the bodily basis of meaning, imagination and reason. University of Chicago Press

Johnson M (2013) The body in the mind: the bodily basis of meaning, imagination, and reason. University of Chicago Press, Chicago

Joy A, Sherry JF Jr (2003) Speaking of art as embodied imagination: a multisensory approach to understanding aesthetic experience. J Consum Res 30(2):259–282

Kaag J (2014) Thinking through the imagination: aesthetics in human cognition. OUP, New York

Kosslyn SM, Thompson WL, Ganis G (2006) The case for mental imagery. Oxford University Press, New York

Lai VT, Curran T (2013) ERP evidence for conceptual mappings and comparison processes during the comprehension of conventional and novel metaphors. Brain Lang 127(3):484–496. https://doi.org/10.1016/j.bandl.2013.09.010

Lai VT, Howerton O, Desai RH (2019) Concrete processing of action metaphors: evidence from ERP. Brain Res 1714:202. https://doi.org/10.1016/j.brainres.2019.03.005

Lakoff G, Johnson M (1999) Philosophy in the flesh. Basic Books, New York

Leslie, AM (1987) Pretense and representation: the origins of "theory of mind." Psych Rev 94(4):412–26

Leslie AM (1994) Pretending and believing: issues in the theory of ToMM. Cognition 50(1–3):211–238

Merleau-Ponty M (1962) Phenomenology of perception. Routledge & Kegan Paul, London

Mithen SJ (1996) The prehistory of the mind a search for the origins of art, religion and science

Mithen SJ (2006) The singing Neanderthals: the origins of music, language, mind and body. Weidenfeld & Nicholson, London, 2005. ISBN 0-297-64317-7

Newson J, Newson E (1968) Four years old in an urban community. George Allen & Unwin, London

Nichols S (2004) Imagining and believing: the promise of a single code. J Aesthet Art Critlsm 62(2):129–139

Nichols S (2006) Imaginative blocks and impossibility: an essay in modal psychology. Arch Imagin, pp 237–255

Nichols S, Stich SP (2000) A cognitive theory of pretense. Cognition 74(2):115–147

Nichols S, Stich SP (2003) Mindreading: an integrated account of pretense, self-awareness, and understanding other minds. Clarendon Press/Oxford University Press, Oxford

O'Connor KP, Aardema F (2005) The imagination: cognitive, pre-cognitive, and meta-cognitive aspects. Conscious Cogn 14(2):233–256

Oatley K, Johnson-Laird PN (1996) The communicative theory of emotions: empirical tests, mental models, and implications for social interaction

Oxman R (2002) The thinking eye: visual re-cognition in design emergence. Des Stud 23(2):135–164

Pelaprat E, Cole M (2011) Minding the gap: imagination, creativity, and human cognition. Integr Psychol Behav Sci Springer, 45:397–418

Perner J (1991) Understanding the representational mind. The MIT Press

Racanière S, Weber T, Reichert D, Buesing L, Guez A, Rezende DJ, Badia AP, Vinyals O, Heess N, Li Y, Pascanu R (2017) Imagination-augmented agents for deep reinforcement learning. In: Advances in neural information processing systems, pp 5690–5701

Rorty R (1967) The linguistic turn. University of Chicago Press, Chicago

Rothbaum BO, Hodges L, Kooper R, Opdyke D, Williford JS, North M (1995) Virtual reality graded exposure in the treatment of acrophobia: a case report. Behav Ther 26:547–554

Rothbaum BO, Hodges L, Watson BA, Kessler GD, Opdyke D (1996) Virtual reality exposure therapy in the treatment of fear of flying: a case report. Behav Res Ther 34:477–481

Schacter DL, Addis DR (2007) The cognitive neuroscience of constructive memory: remembering the past and imagining the future. Philos Trans R Soc Lond B Biol Sci 362(1481):773–786

Schacter DL, Addis DR, Hassabis D, Martin VC, Spreng RN, Szpunar KK (2012) The future of memory: remembering, imagining, and the brain. Neuron 76(4):677–694

Schacter DL, Gaesser B, Addis DR (2013) Remembering the past and imagining the future in the elderly. Gerontology 59(2):143–151

Sheets-Johnstone M (2009) On the challenge of language experience. The corporeal turn: an interdisciplinary reader

Singer DG, Singer JL (2007) Imagination and play in the electronic age, 1st edn. Harvard University Press, Cambridge, Mass

Sirigu A, Duhamel J-R, Cohen L, Pillon B, Dubois B, Agid Y (1996) The mental representation of hand movements after parietal cortex damage. Science 273:1564–1568

Skinner BF (1974) Walden two. Hackett Publishing, Indianapolis

Speer NK, Reynolds JR, Swallow KM, Zacks JM (2009) Reading stories activates neural representations of visual and motor experiences. Psychol Sci 20(8):989–999

Strawson PF (1970) Imagination and perception. In: Foster L, Swanson JW (eds) On experience and theory Amherst. University of Massachusetts Press, MA, pp 31–54

Stumm S, Scott H (2019) Imagination links with schizotypal beliefs, not with creativity or learning. Br J Psychol. https://doi.org/10.1111/bjop.12369

Taylor M (1999) Imaginary companions and the children who create them. Oxford University Press on Demand

Tulving E (2002a) Chronesthesia: conscious awareness of subjective time. In: Principles of frontal lobe

Tulving E (2002b) Episodic memory: from mind to brain. Annu Rev Psychol 53(1):1–25

Vygotsky LS (2004) Voobrazhenie i tvorchestvo v detskom vozraste (Imagination and creativity in childhood) [English trans M.E. Sharpe, Inc., from the Russian text (Moscow: Prosveshchenie, 1967)]. Journal of Russian & East European Psychology, 42(1):7–97. https://www.marxists.org/archive/vygotsky/works/1927/imagination.pdf. Accessed 7 May 2019

Vygotsky LS (1930/1990) Imagination and creativity in childhood (trans. F. Smolucha) Soviet Psychology 28(1):84–96

Wagoner B, Bresco de Luna I (2017) The psychology of imagination: history, theory and new research

Wagoner B, Bresco de Luna I, Awad SH (2017) The Psychology of Imagination: history, theory and new research horizons, IAP

Walton KL (1990) Mimesis as make-believe: on the foundations of the representational arts. Harvard University Press

Watson JB (1928) The ways of behaviorism. Harper, New York

Weber T, Racanière S, Reichert DP, Buesing I., Guez A, Rezende DJ, Badia AP, Vinyals O, Heess N, Li Y, Pascanu R (2017) Imagination-augmented agents for deep reinforcement learning. arXiv: 1707.06203

Yoo J, Kim M (2014) The effects of online product presentation on consumer responses: a mental imagery perspective. J Bus Res 67(11):2464–2472

Chapter 2
The Farthings of Imagination

Chapter Thumbnail

Imagination is difficult to define, particularly in the absence of any consideration of its application and we argue that it is essential to understanding what it is used for, so, let us begin there.

A farthing (*fēorthing*) means a fourth part or a quarter in the Old Northumbrian (an ancient dialect of English) so we propose dividing imagination into four and to consider how each part is employed.

Unlike Mithen, we propose that the most immediate use of imagination is to anticipate and understand what will happen to us next, tomorrow, next year or if we are about to embark on an expedition to the tundra of Siberia.

The second farthing enables us to understand the intentions and behaviour of other people as it is the basis of our Theory of Mind. We assume predicting what is likely to happen next offers a greater advantage than simply being able to function socially. These two farthings probably enable us to cope with the world. The next two farthings are more culturally oriented and serve to support our abilities to generate and understand stories and to be creative. All cultures comprise, more than anything else, stories. These stories tell us who we are, where we are from and where we are going and without the means of understanding this, we are lost. And we so prize creativity, of course, because it enables us to see the world in new and unexpected ways (and according to some commentators is the most valued of all human attributes—apart from our abilities in time-travelling, mind reading, and storytelling that is). All four farthings rely on what Currie and Ravenscroft call *recreative* imagination which is the ability to experience or think about the world from different perspectives. In all, imagination provides us the means to shift perspective and while this is undoubtedly not the whole story, it is key to the operation of these farthings and, we propose goes quite some way to offer the smug reassurance that we are smarter than the other animals.

© Springer Nature Switzerland AG 2020
P. Turner, *Imagination + Technology*, Human–Computer Interaction Series,
https://doi.org/10.1007/978-3-030-37348-1_2

2.1 Introduction

When angry, count to four; when very angry, swear.

Attributed to Mark Twain

Psychology is a science which seeks to establish point-of-view invariant knowledge about how people think, behave, make decisions, emote and so forth which is true of most people, most of the time. And while its achievements have been considerable, the pursuit of this kind of knowledge has tended to either play-down or neglect the role of factors such as context, and other people, or narrative accounts or the fact of our embodiment which would have made its study so much more difficult if not intractable. To these ends psychologists have, for example, sought to study "pure memory" by means of nonsense syllables (uncontaminated by previous learning or associations) never encountered outside a psychology lab or have established that short term memory is very limited in size (e.g. Miller 1956) and much the same is true of the hypothetico-deductive, scientific study of imagination. We have adopted a different approach here and instead explore what we regard as the four most important expressions of imagination. These farthings, we propose, are:

I.   Mental time travelling, by which we regularly anticipate or predict what we might or will do next. We are a future-oriented species, and we spend a good deal of our time and energy worrying about the future, so it is unsurprising that we care about "these make-believe realms of possibility". This manifests as using our imagination to explore such trivia as what we will have for lunch to the unlikely such as "I will buy a yacht when I win the lottery". These mental excursions—forward, backwards (that is by re-experiencing the past), realistically and fictionally—have long been collectively known as "mental time travel" (e.g. Tulving 1984; Suddendorf and Corballis 1997; Soteriou 2018; Beaty et al. 2019).

II. Perhaps the next most important perspective we consider is our ability to use our imaginations to adopt the perspectives of other people—to adopt their point of view. This is a major (or even the) foundation of social cognition and this perspective shifting enables us to create a Theory of Mind which is the name we give to the ability to understand what another person is thinking. (To be pedantic for a moment, most of us have a Theory of Mind which is first and foremost a theory—that is, it is the way we think (theorise or imagine) other people think or imagine.)

III. Storytelling is usually described as imaginative and for good reason as our ability to create a story requires us to adopt the perspectives of others, to see the world as we imagine they would, and for them to interact with others in the story as we imagine they would. Similarly, our ability to understand a story requires us to adopt the perspectives of the people described in the story.

It is difficult to underestimate the importance of stories as, for example, our cultures (that is, the transmission of knowledge, skills and conventions from one generation to the next) comprise, more than anything else, stories. Stories tell us who we are, where we are from and where we are going. Brooks (1984) writes of this as follows, "Our lives are ceaselessly intertwined with narrative, with the stories that we tell and hear told, those we dream or imagine or would like to tell, all of which are reworked in that story of our own lives that we narrate to ourselves in an episodic, sometimes semiconscious, but virtually uninterrupted monologue. We live immersed in narrative, recounting and reassessing the meaning of our past actions, anticipating the outcomes of our future projects, situating ourselves at the intersection of several stories not yet completed."

IV.   Our next contender for how we are different from all the other animals is also our fourth farthing of imagination and it is creativity which is as complex and elusive as imagination itself. Creativity is typically defined in terms of being both original and effective (which may be understood as meaning "being of value"). Recognising that creativity from the perspective of imagination cannot be a complete account of this ability we confine our discussion to how we see the world in unexpected and unconventional ways by way of appropriative reasoning.

Taken together we recognise that each farthing offers coping skills. We discuss the conjunction of farthings at the end of this chapter.

2.2   Mental Time Travel

At the turn of the 19th century, the English essayist William Hazlitt observed that *"The imagination ... must carry me out of myself into the feelings of others by one and the same process by which I am thrown forward as it were into my future being and interested in it"* (1805, p. 3). Here he is writing of two expressions of imagination: the first refers to the feelings of others (which we recognise as "Theory of Mind", and to which we return in the next section) and the second is responsible for "projecting" him into possible futures. We have, of course, already identified this ability as "mental time travel". Mental time travel is our ability to imagine ourselves in our own pasts, and possible futures, but we can mix this up with real and fictional permutations of ourselves (such as "lottery winner") and we can also imagine ourselves in a range of real or fictional locations. Mental time travel is not, of course, "fortune telling" but again reflects our concern with the world and more practically is evident in anticipating a job interview, or the first day of a foreign holiday or a dental appointment.

Evidence from Buckner and Carroll (2007) indicates that we have a "capacity for self-projection" which enables us to mentally shift to "alternate times, places, and perspectives". In using the term "self-projection", they suggest that this prospection requires a shift of perception from the immediate environment to an imagined future environment for oneself. Evidence from their collected self-reports suggest that prospection entails both first-person and third-person perspectives in which one sees oneself. So, where do these speculations about our futures come from? Well,

Table 2.1 Edited from Buckner and Carroll (2007, p. 50)

	Episodic memory	Theory of mind (see next section)	Prospection (i.e. time travel)
Orientation	Past	Present or future	Future
Perceived as	True past event	Another person's viewpoint	Possible future event
Perspective	First person	Another person	First or third person
Function(s)	Remembering	Social cognition	Planning

from our pasts, specifically our memories for similar experiences, from our episodic memories. Episodic memories are our memories of past events, and can involve conceptual content and affective states. Buckner and Carroll conclude that, although it is difficult to establish, it may be that prospection is common and adaptive, and is used productively during decision making, navigation and social cognition. These findings are summarised in Table 2.1.

In addition to this experimental work, there is also evidence from amnesic patients, suffering from severe deficits in episodic memory, who also have difficulties imagining their personal futures or novel scenes. Suddendorf et al. (2009) describes the case of Clive Wearing who suffered an infection which effectively destroyed his hippocampus and left him profoundly amnesic. His amnesia underlines the distinction between semantic memory (which holds knowledge and facts about the world), and episodic memory which holds the details of his past. In *Forever today*, an account written by his wife (Wearing 2005), it is described how he has retained a normal vocabulary, recognizes his family, and can still play the piano. However, his episodic memory is profoundly disrupted and he quickly forgets about things he has just spoken about or experienced only moments earlier. This leaves him with the continual impression that he has just woken up. This and related studies have led Schacter et al. (2007) to propose the "constructive episodic simulation hypothesis" which argues that a critical function of episodic memory is to support the construction of imagined future events based on past experiences, and the flexible recombination of elements of past experiences, into simulations of possible future scenarios. Episodic memory has also been proposed as providing support for the imaginative simulations of how the future might unfold (e.g. Schacter et al. 2007, 2012, 2013). So, how do we travel in time and space without a yet-to-be-invented technology? The simplest answer is through the imaginative manipulation of our episodic memory. We, thus, understand and anticipate the future by manipulating our experiences of the past. Thus, we are living embodiments of Santayana's admonition, "Those who cannot remember the past are condemned to repeat it".

The experiential nature of episodic memory

Episodic memory is our memory for events (Tulving 1972, 1984). Experimental work has revealed that we do not just recall these events, but we re-experience them and it is this which makes them distinct from other kinds of memory. Not only are our memories about our pasts but they are accompanied by our feeling of remembering, whereas other knowledge that we acquire is often purely factual, without any associated personalised "past-ness" attached to it (Downham 2009).

Indeed, the great William James himself recognised that the importance of this when he wrote more than a century ago that, "Memory requires more than the mere dating of a fact in the past. It must be dated in my past." (1890/1950, p. 650). It is for this reason that Tulving made this distinction between remembering and knowing. While we all remember that Paris is the capital of France and we can know this without travelling there and we can know this without remembering how we know this. I can also remember the last time I had a good lunch there (which is more of a challenge than it once was), what I had to eat and with whom I enjoyed it. When I recall this, I can also see (imagine) myself in the scene and fragments of the restaurant's décor (and the stuffed stork in reception). Episodic memory also has an additional dimension, that is, we know that we experienced this specific event at some point in our past (Tulving 1984).

This point is highlighted by Wollheim (1984) who has also observed that the episodic—semantic memory division may correspond to the differences in the way these kinds of remembering are reported. Semantic remembering is of the form, I remember that X happened. In contrast, episodic remembering is more a matter of I remember X happening. Episodic memories are not just a list of facts but resemble the experiences they represent. When an experience is remembered, this memory comprises how things looked, sounded like, or smelled like too. In addition, we also may recall our thoughts and state of mind, our beliefs and feelings (ibid, p. 64). Downham (2009) has also suggested that when we remember events, the remember-er re-enacts the thoughts, feelings, and intentions which they experienced at that time too, and it is these components which make up the first-person perspective. These accompanying qualities may be evidence of what Wollheim calls the intentionality of mental phenomena "that allows them to be internally related to one another or that makes for what has been called the holism of the mental" (1984, p. 37). For Wollheim, the intentionality of episodic memory is the narrative glue which creates a stream of consciousness rather than remembering the past as a series of fragments. This narrative glue, we propose, may also be known as imagination.

From another perspective, Conway (2001) also tells us that that episodic memory is "experience-near" and contrasts it with the "experience-distant" memories of fantasy or plans. He conceives of episodic memory as a system that contains information which is highly event specific and sensory-perceptually detailed. Underlining this, he writes that episodic memories hold records of goal completion, for example, we remember if we have taken a coffee break or brushed our teeth or whether we had abandoned those plans. These memories represent knowledge of the specific actions and the results of those actions derived from "moment-to-moment experience". Conway also presents evidence that episodic memories are represented in those parts of the brain "most closely involved with the processing that took place during the actual experiences" (ibid, 1376).

In spite of the dissociation between semantic and episodic memory, there must be some links between them. The encoding of episodic memories must to some extent depend on semantic memories that are already in place (Tulving 2002a, b); a remembered visit to a restaurant, for example, must depend in part on one's knowledge of what a restaurant is and what happens there. Indeed, descriptions of episodic memories and future simulations comprise both episodic and semantic details that are woven together into a narrative of the experience (e.g. Levine et al. 2002; Addis et al. 2008). Individual episodes, having drawn on semantic elements, are then related to the self in subjectively sensed time. This allows the experience of an event to be stored separately from the semantic system, and retrieved in what Tulving called 'episodic retrieval mode' (Tulving 2002a, b). Just as they are during encoding, retrieved episodic memories are interwoven with elements of semantic memory. The episodic details of an event are not retrieved in isolation of the context that semantic information can provide (Levine et al. 2002). This would apply, we suggest, not only to the reconstruction of past events, but also to the construction of future ones, and even to story-telling—the construction of fictional episodes that permeate folklore, literature, stage drama, film and television (Hassabis et al. 2007; Suddendorf and Corballis 2007).

Finally, it would be misleading to suppose that we can neatly remember and re-experience events from our past veridically. As Ye et al. (2014) have noted, we are all prone to mind-wandering, that is, imagining ourselves elsewhere doing whatever, past or future or whenever, and that this has been reported as a prominent feature in healthy adults across populations. Mind-wandering can then be interwoven with make-believe conversations or events, and the creation of possible worlds, while engaging in mental time-travel.

2.3 Theory of Mind

The second part of William Hazlitt's description of imagination, refers to "the feelings of others" and as we have already suggested this involves (at least in part) imaginatively shifting perspective from one's own point of view to that of other people. But to what end? There is a broad consensus that being able to understand (that is, to interpret, anticipate and respond to) the behaviour and intentions of others is a necessary condition for social interaction.

This ability has several different names but probably the most common is "Theory of Mind" or *ToM* (Premack and Woodruff 1978) though Whiten (1991) calls it "mind-reading"; Dennett (1987) calls it the "intentional stance" while Wellman (1990) describes it as "folk psychology". Indeed, we have several metaphors to describe this ability such as being able to "see or look through another's eyes" or "put on or stand in someone (else's) shoes".

These expressions aside, are we really justified in claiming that we can read the mind of another? Baron-Cohen (1997) writing from an evolutionary perspective, offers the following vignette in support of these frequently anecdotal proposals: "*Imagine that you are an early hominid, and that another early hominid offers to groom you and your mate. You need to reason quickly about whether you should let him approach [...] Making inferences about whether his motives are purely altruistic or whether he might be deceitful is a reasoning strategy that you can apply in time to react to a social threat*" (p. 25). Our own Theory of Mind allows us to infer that the hominid's mindreading provides him with information about the intentions of others, necessary to act quickly and appropriately. From this articulated perspective, Theory of Mind can be recognised as an essential ability for making sense of and surviving in the world.

It is also likely that we share this ability with a number of other social animals (such as chimpanzees). Premack and Woodruff (1978) proposed that chimpanzees can also form such theories. Indeed, it is worth reflecting on the details of their most widely cited research for a moment. This involved getting a chimpanzee to watch a series of short video films of a man struggling with bananas. The chimpanzee was denied sight of the dénouement of this struggle and was instead offered a pair of still photographs of possible outcomes. The chimpanzee was then invited to select an outcome and she chose correctly a significant number of times. The researchers, in trying to account for this result, proposed that she had correctly interpreted the human actor's motives or intentions in the struggle and was thus able to infer "purpose or intention, as well as knowledge, thinking, doubt, guessing, pretending, liking and so forth". We share in making an equivalent array of inferences every day too.

In describing this ability, we have adopted what would be recognised as a common-sense account of mind reading, uncontroversial perhaps but not strictly explanatory.

Mentalizing may be the root

Alvin Goodman begins his *Simulating Minds* (2006, p. 3) by observing that the animal kingdom abounds with social species but "Homo sapiens is a particularly social species, and one of its social characteristics is especially striking: reading one another's minds. People attribute to self and others a host of mental states, ranging from beliefs and aspirations to headaches, disappointments, and fits of anger. Other creatures undoubtedly have pains, expectations, and emotions. But having a mental state and representing another individual mentalizing or mindreading, is a second-order activity: it is mind thinking about minds" and Goodman concludes that mentalizing may be the root of our elaborate social nature.

Currently there are two broad and increasingly overlapping accounts of how we actually "mind-read" and these are the imaginatively entitled theory-theory account and mental simulation.

Theory-theory is based on "folk psychology" which itself refers to our common-sense, everyday ability to understand others and cope with the social world. It is assumed to operate by assigning beliefs and desires to humans and other organisms, in order to predict and/or explain their behaviour (Ratcliffe 2006). Thus, for example, Scholl and Leslie (1999, p. 132) specifically define ToM as "to the capacity to interpret, predict, and explain the behaviour of others in terms of their underlying mental states".

In contrast, proponents of the mental simulation account of ToM, essentially note that "imagination recreates the mental states of others" (Currie and Ravenscroft 2002). So, if we were to consider discussing a problem with another, we would use our imaginations to simulating their mental states in our own minds and then imaginatively adopt his or her perspective. Having done so, I would then use my own cognition to simulate what they were thinking.

It is, however, unlikely that we find ourselves walking from one social encounter to another consciously swapping perspectives, not least because this might be rather cognitively demanding and potentially slow. Like most mental activities, perspective shifting is an unconscious and, more or less, an automatic process of which we are not always aware. We can and do, of course, deliberately adopt the perspective of another when circumstances demand, for example, to make sense of an incident ("what was she thinking?") or prior to a job interview ("what will they think of my convictions?") but most of the time we do not.

Communication and bipedalism

Baron-Cohen (1999) has argued that the appearance of a Theory of Mind (ToM) is more important than the development of bipedalism and language, as without it, being able to produce and understand speech would have not be possible. We need a ToM to communicate and cooperate with each other. More explicitly, Baron-Cohen identifies eight different behaviours which depend on a Theory of Mind. We will consider two of these by way of illustration: (1) Intentional communications are those "communicative acts that are produced in order to change the knowledge state of the listener". If I were to tell someone that tea contains anti-oxidants, I am doing so in order to give you new information that I believe you do not have; that you might be interested in; and that this is information you might want. I am trying to change your knowledge state all of which requires a theory of mind. So, to inform others intentionally, one needs a concept that others have minds that can be informed or uninformed. A second example is "repairing failed communication with others" which is indicative of the belief that the listener has not understood the intended message.

Now summarising, behaviours 3–5 inclusive implicate the role of teaching ("the changing the knowledge state of the less knowledgeable listener"); and persuasion (changing someone else's belief about the value of something); or deception ("withholding information from another"); sharing a plan ("a meeting of minds though the word *conspiracy*—literally *breathing together* is more lyrical"); sharing attention ("both people must be aware of the other person being aware of looking at the same target at they are"). And finally, pretending which is different from intentional deception in that the intention is not to mislead or plant a false belief in an audience, but simply to pretend as evidenced in acting on stage.

Theory of Mind and Culture

A ToM has also been proposed as a necessary condition for, and the basis of, no less a construct than culture itself. Bruner, for example, believes that culture comprises inter-personally negotiated symbolic meanings writing "Social realities are not bricks that we trip over or bruise ourselves on when we kick at them, but the meanings that we achieve by the sharing of human cognitions" (Bruner 1982, p. 837). Similarly, in his essay on Agency and Culture, Ratner (2000) notes that "social intentionality is necessary if social life is to occur. Agency must adapt to and promulgate social patterns. Otherwise, there would be no common, stable, or predictable social life."

Anthropological evidence for this stable social life and the origins of culture have been inferred from such things as evidence of ritualised burial, which implies that our ancestors then were concerned with death and with religion. Mithen (1996) has observed that a common feature of all current religions is that a supernatural agency is postulated who can communicate with you and who can be appeased by way of ritual acts. Conceiving this kind of a supernatural agency and the use of ritual depends on a belief in intentional causation rather than purely physical causation. As for the origins of social intentionality, Tomasello (1999, p. 23) writes "In terms of evolution, then, the hypothesis is that human beings built directly on the uniquely primate cognitive adaptation for understanding external relational categories, they just added a small but important twist in terms of mediating forces such as causes and intentions". In all, social intentionality is a basic characteristic of humans.

Empathy

We should also note that in addition to adopting another's perspective, there is also the issue of empathy (which Hazlitt certainly seems to be suggesting). Empathy is usually defined as understanding and sharing feelings with another.

Empathy has attracted interest from range of researchers and commentators, and in the current context, the most relevant are those engaged in inclusive design; participatory design; more generally, empathy building is often described as an initial step in a user-centred design project (see for example, Bennett and Rosner 2019). Virtual reality systems have also been created expressly for the purpose of engendering empathy (e.g. Schutte and Stilinović 2017; Shin 2018).

So, how do we empathise? Do we imagine the feelings of another and if so, just what are these? It is generally regarded that an emotion is a response to someone, something and comprises, it is widely thought, a cognitive component, strictly an appraisal—is this good, bad, pleasant, threating and so forth; and there is an accompanying feeling too—a bodily response, such as goose-bumps, horripilation, perspiration, dry mouth, "butterflies". There may also be a behavioural component, how do we react—run away, pull a weapon, smile, or hide. Simply imagining this and acting as-if is a tall order and is the preserve of professional actors. But there is an alternative.

Mirror neurons

Rizzolatti and Sinigaglia's (2007) *Mirror in the Mind—How our Minds Share Actions and Emotions* offers this alternative. Their interest begins with how we grasp an object and to understand this they have investigated the primary motor cortex. The F5 area of which is not only implicated in planning motor behaviour but, crucially, has access to visual information (unlike other areas of the motor cortex) and here they found, at least in macaque monkeys, what they describe as mirror neurons. A mirror neuron is one which becomes active both when an animal acts and when the animal observes the same action performed by another. Thus, the neuron "mirrors" the behaviour of the other, as though the observer were itself acting. While such neurons have yet to be conclusively observed in humans, activity consistent with them has been found in the human inferior frontal cortex and superior parietal lobe (Iacoboni et al. 1999) and the supplementary motor area and medial temporal cortex (Keysers and Gazzola 2010).

The function of the mirror system continues to be a subject of considerable speculation. Some have argued that mirror neurons may be important for understanding the actions of other people, and for learning new skills by imitation. Ramachandran and Hirstein (1999) proposed a role for them in self-awareness; others have recently speculated that mirror systems may have contributed to our language abilities (e.g. Schippers et al. 2010) while Iacoboni (2005) has suggested that mirror neuron systems in the human may provide the neural basis for empathy. Subsequent work by Praszkier (2016) and Meyza and Knapska (2018) would tend to lend support to this.

2.4   Storytelling

Storytelling must be one of the most prominent expressions of our imaginations and it is likely that we have been telling tales for as long as we have had the cognitive means to do so. Suddendorf et al. (2011), for example, have speculated that human language may have evolved primarily for the communication of such stories, "whether from the past or the imagined future, or indeed in the form of fiction". And Green (2005) argues that narrative is intrinsic to human thinking, citing Schank and Abelson's (1995) assertion that "all knowledge is stories" and psycho-anthropological studies such as Mancuso (1986) who suggests that infants in most cultures acquire a basic narrative grammar by the age of three.

Unsurprisingly then, stories and storytelling have had immeasurable importance to both us individually and collectively. This is nicely illustrated in *The Edge of Memory* (2018) in which Nunn identifies ancient stories and oral traditions from the barely post-glacial world. The stories describe lost coastlines (the seas having risen 70 m since the glaciers retreated) and with this a host of practical information regarding, for example, the location of drinking water and food sources.

However, for the purposes of this discussion, we will focus on only two forms of stories: namely, beginning with those without which we simply would not be and the more familiar fictional stories.

Calvin who quotes Kathryn Morton who writes, "the first sign that a baby is going to be a human being and not a noisy pet comes when he begins naming the world and demanding the stories that connect its parts. Once she knows the first of these he will instruct his teddy bear, enforce his worldview on victims in the sandlot, tell himself stories of what he is doing as he plays and forecast stories of what he will do when he grows up. He will keep track of the actions of others and relate deviations to the person in charge." (Calvin 2006, p. 88). Calvin continues that, our plan ahead abilities develop from these childhood stories and provide the foundation for our ethical choices as we imagine "a course of action, imagine its effects on others and decide not to do it".

About me

This first category of storytelling comprises our personal histories, our "autobiographies" and while these are unlikely to be serialised in the Sunday press, we are all too aware of the consequences of suffering deficits to such memories (*cf.* Alzheimer's disease). Our autobiographies are those stories we tell ourselves to explain why we are married to him or her; or are working as the CFO for a multi-national pharmaceutical or on the cheese counter of a 7–11; and why we are keen on amateur dramatics, or collecting spores, mould and fungus.

Conway and Pleydell-Pearce's (2000) model of autobiographical memory is based on our experiences which are retained as a whole raft of episodic memories (which as we have already seen are the building blocks of mental time travel and imagination as a whole). Indeed, autobiographical memory is not just those memories relevant to oneself, it is, according to Conway (2001) "a transitory mental representation: it is a temporary but stable pattern of activation across the indices of the autobiographical memory knowledge base that encompasses knowledge at different levels of abstraction, including event-specific sensory perceptual details, very often—although by no means always—in the form of visual mental images".

The structure of autobiographical memory as proposed by Conway and Rubin (1993) has identified three types (or strata) of autobiographical memory, namely, lifetime periods, general events and event specific knowledge (illustrated below). Of these, the first category is the least relevant to the current discussion but may be thought of in terms of memories "when I was a child", "memories of being at university "and so forth. General events are more specific than and more heterogeneous than lifetime periods. Conway describes general events as encompassing both repeated events (treating a patient, giving a lecture, going to work) and single events (seeing a rare form of cancer, giving the keynote at CHI) and he also writes that they may also represent "mini-histories" such as learning to drive a car which may contain a number of vivid memories related to specific goal-attainments (first time driving solo, first run-in with the police) (Fig. 2.1).

Bluck (2003) identifies three functions of autobiographical memory as concerning the self, its role in maintaining social relations and its directive function. Of the first

Fig. 2.1 Autobiographical memory (redrawn from Conway 1995, p. 68)

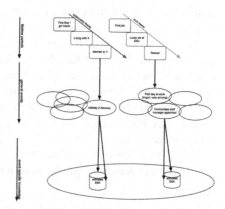

she writes, "knowledge of the self in the past, and as projected into the future has been seen as one critical type of self-knowledge". She also notes that Conway regards autobiographical memory as contributing to the self in terms of its continuity and development. A further, hypothesised function is the personal past may preserve a sense of being a coherent person over time. Bluck, like Neisser, regards the most important role of autobiographical memory as having a social function. This social function primarily maintains social relationships through the exchange of personal stories and memories. Finally, he also notes that autobiographical memory has a directive function too, particularly with respect to problem solving (old information being used to solve current problems); and more generally to use previous experience as a means of directing or predicting the results of future behaviour for both ourselves and others. Conway has, perhaps more than any other researcher, created an account of memory in which personal goals are an important component. These goals not only contribute to the creation of new memories but also to their maintenance and retrieval (Conway 2001, p. 1376).

Finally, it should be noted that Conway's description of autobiographical memory is in terms of an "episodic memory database". We contrast this with what Bruner describes as making experience meaningful. These employs "the side of the mind" that leads to good stories, gripping drama, primitive myths and rituals, and plausible historical accounts or what he calls the "narrative mode". Bruner regards this mode of operation "world making" which he describes as the principal function of mind,

This seems to imply that our autobiographies are constructed, and should not be treated as a simple record of what happened. Instead, it is a continuing interpretation and reinterpretation of our experiences.

Fictional stories

Of the more expected form of a fictional story, a great deal has been written of them and why we tell them, so much so that any attempt at a summary as a part of a chapter in this slim volume is unrealistic. However, we do begin by borrowing the opening quotation from Booker's (2004, p. 1) major work where he writes, "… to show how small a quality of REAL FICTION there is in the world; and that the same images, with very little variation, have served all the authors who have ever written.[1]" By images, Booker means plots of which he has counted only seven. So, of all the millions of stories in the world, research reveals that there are only seven (7) plots and an uncountable number of "riffs" on these basic themes.

We cannot know when the first story was told, nor who told it to whom but what seems more likely is that the oldest stories may have involved acting out a myth which may be well known to the audience, or perhaps it was an incident or scene, real or imagined, from the life of a god, spirit or hero or just the late king. These stories may also have been "told" without recourse to language. A very early form of story may have been in the form of a pictogram, and one such candidate is the "Shaft Scene" (dated to 15000 BCE) which was found at the Lascaux cave system in France. The pictogram was found at the deepest, most awkward to reach part of the entire cave and depicts a fight between a bison and a man. The bison lies dead as it

---

[1] The quotation is from Boswell's *Life of Johnson* and the capitalisation is in the original.

has been speared and is next to a man who has a bird-like head (he is thought to be a psychopomp—one who escort the souls of the dead) and lying next to him is a bird on a pole. While we may not know what this all means, we nonetheless recognise it as a story.

More evidence of the great age of stories comes from Da Silva and Tehrani (2016) who have presented evidence from their phylogenetic analysis of the development of Indo-European languages to suggest that several common fairy stories date from the Bronze Age.[2] The fairy stories predate English, French and Italian and it is likely that they probably were told in an extinct Indo-European language. The authors found themselves agreeing with the work of Wilhelm Grimm (him of Grimm's fairy tales) whose research revealed that some of these stories go back much further than the earliest literary record and indeed further back than Classical mythology—some versions of these stories appear in Latin and Greek texts—but our findings suggest they are much older than that. Jack and the Beanstalk, for example, dates from a group of stories classified as The Boy Who Stole Ogre's Treasure and can be traced back to when Eastern and Western Indo-European languages split about than 5,000 years ago. While "The Smith and the Devil" which is a story about a blacksmith who sells his soul to the Devil was estimated to be 6,000 years old. Although it is not a well-known story, Faust would have recognised it. We also know that Jack and the Beanstalk is more than 5000 years old whereas Beauty and the Beast and Rumpelstiltskin are a mere 4,000 years old.

Fairy stories often have themes common to humans throughout the world and through all ages, such as family, betrayal, violence and survival. However, we can more generally define a story as a narrative account of events that may involve the past, present, future and make-believe events (cf. mental time travelling). Stern (1997) has also described them as a repository of all human knowledge and writes that "stories uniquely present both our beliefs and our knowledge about the world" which underlines the role of imagination as a sense-making mechanism.

For the sake of consistency with the next chapter, let us treat some stories (which we dub "scaffolded stories") as comprising two parts, namely the imaginative, make-believe and a prop or props.

The imaginative, make-believe aspect is articulated or crystallized with and through the prop. So, for example, a potentially very early prop is the Warka Vase which is decorated with a narrative of the presentation of offerings to the goddess Inanna (Fig. 2.2). This may have served to trigger, prompt, remind or scaffold the telling of the story of the Sacred Marriage between a deity and a mortal, thus elevating the status of the latter. Further examples, have been revealed from the analysis of oral storytelling which revealed the presence of "formulas" such as "the wine-dark sea," or the "rosy-fingered dawn" (Lord 1960/1991). These formulas serve lend structure and to pace the story. Lord also identified what he describes as "themes" which are common to many stories such as the "rule of three" which also help structure

---

[2]Dating the Bronze age depends upon which part of the world we are discussing. In the Near East it is dated between 3200–1200 BC or approximately 5200–3200 years ago. However, in China, it was about 1000 years later.

Fig. 2.2 The Warka Vase (https://commons.wikimedia.org/wiki/File:Warka_vase_(background_retouched).jpg). CC BY-SA 4.0

a story—Goldilocks and the three bears, the offer of three wishes from a magickal creature, or the house building exploits of the three little pigs or the adventures of the three animals of Bremen.

The default network

In addition to these structures and props, stories are a product of the imagination, which as we have seen so far, often relies on re-hashing or re-presenting experiences we have had but in new(ish) ways. One other source of which lies with the brain's default network (Ingvar 1974, 1979, 1985). The default network is a network of highly correlated, interacting regions of the brain and is found to be active when a person is not focused on the outside world and the brain is at wakeful rest, such as during daydreaming. It is also active when the individual is thinking about others, thinking about themselves (retrieving autobiographical memories), remembering the past, and planning for the future (e.g., Buckner et al. 2008; Raichle et al. 2001). Since its identification, this default circuit has been of interest to those who were concerned to know why the brain was consuming more oxygen and glucose when it was at rest than when it was apparently busy (e.g., Raichle et al. 2001).

Gruberger and his colleagues tell us that, "Mind-wandering is among the most robust and permanent expressions of human conscious awareness, classically regarded by philosophers, clinicians, and scientists as a core element of an intact sense of self". Prospective mind-wandering, that is, imagining ourselves in the future, has also been reported as a prominent feature in healthy adults across populations (Ye et al. 2014). Mind-wandering can then be seen as interwoven with make-believe conversations or events, the creation of possible worlds, and engaging in "mental time-travel". Gruberger and his colleagues tell us that, "Mind-wandering is among the most robust and permanent expressions of human conscious awareness, classically regarded by philosophers, clinicians, and scientists as a core element of an intact sense of self".

Mind-wandering is internally directed cognition that occurs when our thoughts turn from the current task to become preoccupied with unrelated memories, imagination, fantasies, plans, feelings, or with unsolved problems.

Buckner et al. (2008) have proposed that it may be the source of internally directed cognition such as the creation and examination of autobiographical memories, speculations about the future which are separate from the real world. Pace-Schott (2013, p. 1) has also suggested that this is a credible source for night-time dreams, writing that *"dreams create new stories out of nothing. Although dreams contain themes, concerns, dream figures, objects, etc., that correspond closely to waking life, these are only story elements."* He then goes on to argue that this story-like structure found in dreams may have become integrated into existing belief systems, or even to create new beliefs and legends.

Telling stories

Neil Gaiman describes his work as a novelist as, "I make things up and write them down" (amazon). While Oliver Postgate and Peter Firmin who created the children's TV series The Clangers, Bagpuss and (the greatest) Noggin the Nog described their working relationship as, "He [Postgate] wrote and imagined things and I brought them to life as pictures".

Currie (1990, p. 18) does say a little more, and argues that for text to count as fiction it must be the result of fictive intention. The unfamiliar word fictive means "formed by the imagination" so, for example, to describe your father's best friend as an uncle is a fictive relationship. The fictive intention of the author of a story is for the reader to make-believe its contents, "what the author of a fiction does intend is that the reader takes a certain attitude towards the propositions uttered during his performance. This is the attitude of "imaginative involvement" which means believing a story to be true. Our imaginations also liberate us from the real world by adopting a fictional perspective which underpins game playing and (arguably) the experience of telepresence in virtual reality. Currie, among others, calls this imaginative involvement. While some researchers have argued that we have "suspended our disbelief" in such circumstances (e.g. Coleridge 1817), we propose that an equally plausible alternative is that we actively make-believe with the novel or movie—we co-create our own story rather than maintaining the uncomfortable double negative "I know that this is not so, but I suspend my disbelief". Indeed designers, artists and writers have long been aware of the power of their media to engage the individual.

Understanding stories

Individually, Searle and Currie and Walton and Byrne and Booker have all emphasized that authors invite the readers to believe their stories to be "true". Searle (1975), for example, tells us that stories are episodes of "intended playful pretense" where the act of pretending is shared between reader and author, and narratives "publicly function as props in a game of make-believe". Although the nature and operation of fictional logic is deeply contested in philosophy and literary theory, most accounts of the nature of fiction and "truth in fiction" argue for the role of pretence and make-believe (e.g. Currie 1990; Goodman 2011; Gatzia and Sotnak 2014).

Byrne (2007) argues that authors invite readers to "make-believe that certain propositions are true". While Currie asserts that "the author who produces a work of fiction is engaged in a communicative act, an act that involves having a certain kind of intention: the intention that the audience shall make-believe the content of the story that is told" (Currie 1990, p. 24). Take, for example, the James Bond stories that feature a character who joined the Royal Navy reserves in 1941 but remains astonishingly spry 78 years later. As I write there is some speculation that Bond is to become gender-fluid and may appear in future movies as a woman.

2.5   Creativity

Evidence that imagination and creativity are closely related, or are inter-dependent, or are synergetic or are near-enough synonyms can be found across the study of creativity with writers such as Folkmann (2013) describing imagination as a "creative force". In a similar vein, Pelaprat and Cole (2011) propose that imagination and creativity have a 'cyclical' relationship that is mediated by experience and knowledge. Experience shapes imagination, and imagination contributes to creative activity. If the output of creative activity is "perceived as new the products of imagination become creative when they enter the cultural world of interaction." This and "creative force" clearly show that the level of discourse on this is given to primarily to the impressionistic. In this book we treat creativity quite narrowly as imaginatively *seeing-as*.

Kaski (2002) writes that we can entertain the notion of imagination offering us a "creative perspective" on the world—one of seeing the world differently—and reminds us of the American cubist sculptor, Jacques Lipchitz who described his own practice as "Cubism is like standing at a certain point on a mountain and looking around. If you go higher, things will look different; if you go lower, again they will look different. It is a point of view."

Creativity is typically defined as the generation of original, appropriate, useful, and valuable ideas, products, or solutions (e.g. Sternberg and Lubart 1999; Schmajuk et al. 2009; Hennessey and Amabile 2010) Tellingly, these three sources cited here do not agree with each other on the makeup of creativity, as like imagination it has a slippery and elusive quality. While Batey and Furnham (2006) observe that creativity is highly valued, they also note that *"psychological research regarding creativity remains an academic backwater"* (p. 355), so here is something else that it has in common with imagination.

From an unexpected perspective, Kaag (2014) writes of CS Peirce's interest in creativity in "great men", that is, in those who had exhibited extraordinary imagination which evidenced their "genius". Peirce argued creative imagination was not confined to the Arts but could also be found in the Sciences too heralding, perhaps, the recognition of scientific imagination. Kaag suspects that this association may have begun with Vygotsky who differentiated the functioning of creative imagination between adults and children. The key difference is rooted in the level of maturity of the individuals involved. Vygotsky argued that a child's experience is relatively simple, elementary, and generally just down-right poor compared with that of an adult's which is correspondingly subtler, complex, and diverse. He also observed that "the convergence of intellect and imagination is a distinctive characteristic of development in adolescence" (Vygotsky 1931/1991, p. 83). Thus, he argues, full imagination only becomes fully available in adulthood, further he tells us that imagination is special in that it is, "... *a new formation that is not present in the consciousness of the very raw young child, is totally absent in animals, and represents a specifically human form of conscious activity.*" He ends by observing that that "*imagination in adolescence is, from the developmental point of view, the successor of children's play*" (p. 77).

Finally, Ferguson (1992) offers an unusual perspective on the notion of creativity at least with respect to engineering. In his *Engineering and the Mind's Eye*, he notes that the idea of creativity blossomed in the 1950s, and was intended to describe the ability of some people to synthesize new ideas from combinations disparate experiences. While this might seem an uncontroversial definition but he goes on to describe how it was trivialized as a fad "[…] that swept through the (US) engineering schools of the late 1950s", which he believes was in response to the post-Sputnik period of public hysteria. Creativity was thus encouraged to achieve or regain dominance over the Soviets in engineering and weapon development.

Creativity as imagination

Another source of creative thought which may be shared with imagination may originate with "mind wandering" and the so-called default network (already described in Sect. 2.4). This proposal has some measure of experimental support coming from the studies of facilitating creativity by effectively not thinking about it—it being the primary task demanding creativity to solve or complete it (e.g. Baird et al. 2012). These interruptions are described as incubation periods and are characterised as periods of undemanding work (e.g. washing the dishes) which enable the mind to wander.

Thus, we propose that mind wandering may also be an important source of creative imagination too. The default network in the brain, as discussed earlier, is a distinct neural system that is active when we are not focused on a task (e.g. Buckner et al. 2008; Raichle et al. 2001). Studies have suggested that the default mode network is active during mind-wandering and daydreaming, the consideration of oneself and understanding others, retrieving autobiographical memories, and imagining the future. As this 'state of mind' is our default condition, it consequently stands to reason that these forms of mind-wandering are important to creativity, planning, and the understanding of ourselves in relation to others (e.g., Buckner et al. 2008; McVay and Kane 2010; Mooneyham and Schooler 2013). This planning may offset some of the performance drawbacks of mind wandering as it can prepare an individual to cope with expected events, and imagining potential outcomes could reduce vulnerability and improve readiness. Our primary interest in the default network is its role in mind-wandering, which is a potential source of stimuli for creative make-believe.

Imagination and abductive reasoning

Abduction is the third form of reasoning which exists alongside the more familiar forms, deduction and induction. Deductive reasoning begins with a premise, then a second premise, and finally an inference. So, for example: all men are mortal, he is a man therefore he is mortal. If the premises are true then the conclusions are true. By contrast, with inductive reasoning we move from instances to generalisations, for example, it has been observed that the sun rose this morning and the day before that and the day before that (…), therefore the sun will rise tomorrow morning. We have strong evidence of the sun's behaviour so, we can be confident that it will be probably the case tomorrow. Abductive reasoning, by contrast, is used by medical practitioners in examining a patient, or a juror in murder trial or a scientist making sense of their data. Unlike deduction and induction, imagination is said to be required to formulate a diagnosis, verdict or hypothesis respectively. If we consider the paradox at the heart of problem solving we can, perhaps see the place of imagination in abduction. For us to solve a problem, we must know what the answer might look like and that takes an act of imagination. As Peirce (1898) writes, "When a man desires ardently to know the truth, his first effort will be to imagine what that truth can be. He cannot prosecute his pursuit long without finding that imagination unbridled is sure to carry him off the track. Yet nevertheless, it remains true that there is, after all, nothing but imagination that can ever supply an inkling of the truth. He can stare stupidly at phenomena; but in the absence of imagination they will not connect themselves in any rational way". Douven (2017) describes abduction as a "type of inference that is frequently employed, in some form or other, both in everyday and in scientific reasoning". And according to Peirce (2002), abduction is the only way to arrive at a new idea. Abductive reasoning, however, is not limited to everyday contexts. Quite the contrary: philosophers of science have argued that abduction is a cornerstone of scientific methodology; with Williamson (2017) writing "The abductive methodology is the best science provides, and we should use it".

Stimulating imagination
Perhaps underlining the mysterious nature of imagination, and despite the value and importance we place on creativity, research has been pursued not so much to understand the "architecture" or dynamics of creativity but to develop methods of improving its quantity and quality (with or without a Soviet threat). So, descriptions (and promotions) of children's toys and artistic digital technology are often expressed in terms of supporting or promoting imagination (and incidentally giving your children a much needed head start at school).

However, the psychological evidence suggests that the best way to encourage imagination and/or creativity is by not being creative or imaginative and by allowing the mind to wander (e.g., Gilhooly et al. 2013; Dijksterhuis and Meurs 2006).

In addition to mental time travel which offers a personal prediction of one's own future, more general and societal predictions are the domain of creative imagination. I have a copy of *Being Human: Human-computer Interaction in the year 2020* which offers such predictions and as I write 2020 is only a few weeks away. The book is copyrighted 2008 and was edited by four well respected experts in HCI. The core material for the book was generated at a Microsoft sponsored forum in 2007 attended by a broad mix of researchers and specialists tasked with answering the question that became the title of the book.

The predictions have proved to be fairly accurate but were broad enough not to miss their mark too often however and as usual I could find no mention of imagination or make-believe. Predicting what the rapidly changing technological world will be like in 12–13 years is one which is based on imagination, or what-if thinking or abductive thinking (which has imagination at its heart, see Sect. 2.5) or letting our minds wander (see Sect. 2.4) and not to mention at least one of these is odd. But in common with most of HCI, imagination does not appear to be on anyone's agenda.

As this kind of prediction is so fraught with difficulties it is even more surprising that the contributors would not seek to leverage their *technological imaginations* so as to improve their chances of getting our predictions right.

Vygotsky, who coined the term, defines a psychological tool as something which enables the operation of our basic psychology, such as memory, attention or imagination, to operate in new—extended ways. More recently, Kozulin (1998) defines psychological tools as *"the symbolic cultural artifacts—signs, symbols, texts, formulae, and most fundamentally, language—that enable us to master psychological functions like memory, perception, and attention in ways appropriate to our cultures"*. This again is an appeal to distributed cognition but the explicit introduction of the word "cultural" changes this.

Our interest is in those psychological/cultural tools which extend, and leverage our imaginations. In Gold's *The Plenitude* (2007) we find a discussion of two interesting ideas, first off is the proposal that the Plenitude exists and that innovation patterns can be found at work within it. The Plenitude is described as a "dense knotted ecology of human-made stuff, which we might rephrase as the technological context within which our imaginations might operate. However, it is the innovation patterns which are of interest here. He writes of them, *"As I am bounded from [...] the four professional arenas of art, science, design and engineering, I found there was actually a shared and limited set of methodologies for the creation of new stuff. These seven methods or patterns are used by all four disciplines, but are differently weighted in each area"*. He suggests that these patterns when "every so often you come to your desk, your workbench, your design table and you are stuck. No ideas flow. Everything seems already invented that needed to be invented. It is at that moment quite helpful to pull out this little list". This list is not only for generating ideas as we can also make sense of a new product. These seven "patterns of innovation" which might serve as psychological tools—and to leverage imagination. These are nothing like as neat (conceptually) as the use of props ... but may serve to guide and scaffold the technological imagination. They are:

1. Find a problem and fix it
2. "It is a thing of genius"
3. The "Big Kahuna"—named after the fictional hamburger chain referenced in "Pulp Fiction"
4. Stuff desires to be better stuff—a reference to the allure of incremental improvements
5. The Future Exists
6. Colonisation

7. Change the Definition

Find a problem and fix it
This pattern of innovation begins with the all too familiar, "I have a problem with…".
Solution—imagine (and design) something which fixes this problem, for example,
"I have a problem remembering where I left my car keys …" Solution—create a set
of smart car keys; build a wearable memory aid; design a car which does not require
keys and so forth. This is, arguably, the easiest approach to innovation and is, of
course, another way of saying "necessity is the mother of invention". However, this
particular pattern highlights the limits of imagination as being directed at a single
and potentially simplistic framed problem. As Gold points out, in 1900 the cities
in the US had a huge problem—horse manure. Horse are nice; and horse can pull
carriages but they do leave great piles of manure everywhere they go. One solution
to this in London, at more or less the same time, was for the affluent to move out of
town to escape the smell and flies associated with this manure. A more egalitarian
solution, however, was the invention of the horse-less carriage but the motor car, as
we have learned, is not a problem free solution. We can easily recognise air pollution
and its effects on people and buildings; the redesign of our cities to accommodate
cars (rather than people) and global warming, and the 1000,000+ killed every year
on the roads. The telephone is another solution to the problem of people wishing
to talk to each other though they are miles apart. When it was first invented it was
envisaged that there would be, perhaps, one or two telephones per town. Indeed, as
little as 60 years ago (in the UK) people did not typically have a telephone in their
homes and had to go a better equipped neighbour or the Post Office to make a call.
Then telephones became one per house; then mobiles were invented and telephony
became ubiquitous and now there are train carriages in which are the use of mobile
phones is prohibited.

"It is a thing of genius"
A second pattern is to imagine something brilliant. This approach has two pre-
requisites: you need to be a genius and a deep personal belief that you are right. Gold
gives us the example of Chester Carlson, who in 1938, invented electrostatic copying.
For the next 6 years Carlson tried to interest a company in his invention without
success. In 1944 a non-profit research group named Battelle Memorial Institute
licensed his idea. In 1947 Xerox bought the license. In 1959–21 years after the original
invention—that Carlson's idea turned into reality in the form of a copy machine A
second example is the creation of the iPod. "With iPod, Apple has invented a whole
new category of digital music player that lets you put your entire music collection in
your pocket and listen to it wherever you go" said Steve Jobs as the first iPod launched
in 2001. "With iPod, listening to music will never be the same again". Neither the
copy machine nor the iPod fixed a known problem and there was no specific need
driving it.

The Future Exists
A consequence of Moore's law is that in the future everything will be smaller, faster,
cheaper. Your smartphone has more memory and computing power than Nasa when

they sent men to the Moon … and in 5 years' time … So, we can design software/media which currently require a supercomputer (movies like Shrek or LotR) but in the future you will be able to do this using your phone … the future does not exist. When the first UbiCom components began to appear, the Web had not been invented which made UbiCom look wrong footed.

Colonisation

The history of popular sports (e.g. baseball, cricket/football etc) generally has the form of:

- In the beginning you play it for free in the garden/yard
- Then it became appropriated, improved upon and people pay money to watch other more skilful people playing it
- Then you watch it for a fee on TV
- Then you play it on your games console.

The processes of this form of innovation are: find something no one owns, improve on it, rationalise it, package it, "gutsy it up", make it smooth and consistent => new product. Examples, Campbell's Home Cookin' Soup—no one owns home-made soup—improve on it, rationalise it, package it, "gutsy it up", make it smooth and consistent => sell home cookin' soup back to people. Water—water is cheap unless someone sells it back to you in a blue bottle.

Change the Definition

Walter Gropius (the founder of Bauhaus) redefined houses as "machine for living" a definition which opens up new ways of thinking about designing for the home, but the best example of this is "Apple reinventing the phone". The Apple CEO Steve Jobs said, "I have been looking forward to this for two and a half years" and then proceeded to introduce the iPhone, which he called a leapfrog product that is much smarter than the previous generation of mobile phones, combining the iPod, mobile phone, 2-megapixel camera and an Internet communicator in one device. In retrospect, it is difficult to appreciate how impressive the technical specification of the original iPhone was, which boasted a 3.5-in., 160-pixel per inch patented touch screen which popped up a soft keyboard for each application. "The software is at least five years ahead of others," Jobs said. iTunes is used to synch all media and data, such as contacts and calendar, to iPhone. The killer app for the phone is making calls, Jobs said. The phone includes, contacts, calendar, visual voice mail, SMS messaging and quad band GSM + Edge, Wi-Fi and Bluetooth. The software enables multiple SMS messaging sessions at once. As an Internet communicator, the iPhone supports rich text email, a fully usable HTML Web browser in Safari, Google Maps, widgets and Wi-Fi. The landscape mode makes reading Web pages much easier and you can "pinch" the screen to resize the page.

Personally, my preferred example is from the TV series Yes Minister. In the episode "Party games" (Jay and Lynn 1984), the men from Brussels threatened to introduce the standardise Euro-sausage to the UK. Europe was unhappy with the UK's recipe and threatened to ban it, describing it as a "high fat, emulsified offal tube". To resolve this problem, it was renamed the "British banger".

Gold suggests that when he gets stuck (and everyone does get stuck) an appeal to one of these patterns often provides the necessary inspiration (for which we can read "creative imagination") to move on.

2.6   On Being Prudent

Prudence is an unexpected topic to encounter at the end of this chapter. To be prudent is to act with care and our imaginations enable us to act this way. In chapter one, we proposed that we imagine because we care, not just because we can, and it is to this point we return. We do not exercise our imagination just because we can but because we need it to make sense of our current situation and to plan for the future. So, what of the four farthings which enable us to act with care?

While we have identified the four farthings of imagination, we have not suggested that the divisions among them are clear cut. They are not. They are all quite distinct, but we recognise that they overlap and may be combined, spliced or made to work in concert. All four share and rely on the imaginative shifting of perspective; and thus, all four are concerned with the manipulation of metaphor.

1. We imagine possible futures (as mental time travel) to ensure that we are ready to cope with what befalls us and to explore alternatives without committing to them;
2. We imagine the point of view others (Theory of Mind) to understand and to participate in social interaction;
3. We imaginatively understand who we are and where we are from (the imaginative creation of autobiographical memory and we understand and learn from the narratives which comprise our culture;
4. We imaginative appropriate tools, technology to solve problems creatively. Our imaginative inspired abductive reasoning allows us to understand the physical world.

So armed, we can use our imaginations to make sense of ourselves, and each other from both individual and cultural perspectives and use it to create and maintain our sense of personal continuity (our sense of self). We use our imagination to integrate past and present experiences giving us the sense of living from one moment to the next, from one day to the next day.

As for prudence proper, here we need to consult Flyvbjerg (2001, p. 57) who wrote, "in sum, the three intellectual virtues (which Aristotle categorised as in The Nicomachean Ethics,) episteme, techne and phronesis[3] can be characterised as follows:

- Episteme. Scientific knowledge. Universal, invariable, context-independent.

---

[3]This is the most unfamiliar of all forms of knowledge and is most easily approached by regarding it as "practical wisdom" or more simply as "prudence".

- Techne. Craft/art. Pragmatic, variable, context-dependent. Oriented towards production.
- Phronesis. Deliberation about values. Context-dependent. Oriented towards action.

He continues, "phronesis is that intellectual virtue most relevant to praxis" (i.e. doing things as opposed to thinking about doing things) and "Phronesis requires interaction between the general and the concrete, it requires consideration, judgment and choice. More than anything else, phronesis requires experience".

At the outset of this chapter we argued that to understand imagination we needed to consider how it is used in practice. As we have shown, all in all this enables us to be prudent.

References

Addis DR, Alana TW, Daniel LS (2008) Age-related changes in the episodic simulation of future events. Psychol Sci 19(1):33–41

Baird B, Smallwood J, Mrazek MD, Kam JW, Franklin MS, Schooler JW (2012) Inspired by distraction: mind wandering facilitates creative incubation. Psychol Sci 23(10):1117–1122

Baron-Cohen S (1997) Mindblindness: an essay on autism and theory of mind. MIT Press, Cambridge, MA

Baron-Cohen S (1999) Evolution of a theory of mind? In: Corballis M, Lea S (eds) The descent of mind: psychological perspectives on hominid evolution. Oxford University Press, Oxford

Batey M, Furnham A (2006) Creativity, intelligence, and personality: a critical review of the scattered literature. Genet, Soc, Gen Psychol Monogr 132(4):355–429

Beaty RE, Seli P, Schacter DL (2019) Thinking about the past and future in daily life: an experience sampling study of individual differences in mental time travel. Psychol Res 83(4):805–816

Bennett CL, Rosner DK (2019) The promise of empathy: design, disability, and knowing the other. In: Proceedings of the 2019 CHI conference on human factors in computing systems. ACM, p 298

Bluck S (2003) Autobiographical memory: exploring its functions in everyday life. Memory 11(2):113–123

Booker C (2004) The seven basic plots: why we tell stories. A&C Black

Brooks P (1984) Reading for the plot: design and intention in narrative. Harvard University Press

Bruner J (1982) The language of education. Soc Res 49:835–853

Buckner RL, Carroll DC (2007) Self-projection and the brain. Trends Cogn Sci 11:49–57

Buckner RL, Andrews-Hanna JR, Schacter DL (2008) The brain's default network: anatomy, function, and relevance to disease. Annu N Y Acad Sci 1124:1–38. https://doi.org/10.1196/annals.1440.011

Byrne RM (2007) The rational imagination: How people create alternatives to reality. MIT press

Calvin WH (2006) Filling the empty niches. AmeriQuests 3(2):55ff

Charles Sanders Peirce (1898) The collected papers. In: Principles of philosophy, vol I

Coleridge ST (1817) Biographia Literaria. https://books.google.co.uk/books/about/Biographia_Literaria.html?id=Q2nB8jpp0LsC&redir_esc=y. Accessed 4 Nov 2018

Conway MA (1995) Flashbulb memories. Erlbaum, Brighton, Sussex, England

Conway MA (2001) Sensory–perceptual episodic memory and its context: Autobiographical memory. Philos Trans R Soc Lond B Biol Sci 356(1413):1375–1384

Conway MA, Pleydell-Pearce CW (2000) The construction of autobiographical memories in the self-memory system. Psychol Rev 107(2):261

Conway MA, Rubin DC (1993) The structure of autobiographical memory. In: Collins AE, Gather-cole SE, Conway MA, Morris PEM (eds) Theories of memory. Erlbaum, Hove, Sussex, England, pp 103–137

Currie, G (1990). The nature of fiction. Cambridge University Press, New York

Currie G, Ravenscroft I (2002) Recreative minds: imagination in philosophy and psychology. OUP University Press, Oxford

Da Silva SG, Tehrani JJ (2016) Comparative phylogenetic analyses uncover the ancient roots of Indo-European folktales. R Soc Open Sci 3(1):150645

Dennett D (1987) The intentionality stance. MIT Press, Cambridge, MA

Dijksterhuis A, Meurs T (2006) Where creativity resides: the generative power of unconscious thought. Conscious Cogn 15(1):135–146

Douven I (2017) Abduction. In: Zalta EN (ed) The Stanford encyclopaedia of philosophy (Summer 2017 edn). https://plato.stanford.edu/archives/sum2017/entries/abduction/

Downham R (2009) Episodic memory as enactive know-how. In: Proceedings of the ASCS09, pp 81–83

Ferguson ES (1992) Engineering and the mind's eye. MIT Press, Cambridge, MA

Flyvbjerg B (2001) Making social science matter: Why social inquiry fails and how it can succeed again. Cambridge University Press

Folkmann MN (2013) The aesthetics of imagination in design. MIT Press, Cambridge, MA

Gatzia DE, Sotnak E (2014) Fictional truth and make-believe. Philosophia 42(2):349–361

Gilhooly KJ, Georgiou G, Devery U (2013) Incubation and creativity: Do something different. Think Reason 19(2):137–149

Goodman A (2006) Simulating minds

Goodman J (2011) Pretense theory and the imported background. Open J Philos 1(1):22–25

Green MC (2005) Transportation into narrative worlds: implications for the self. In: Tesser A, Wood JV, Stapel DA (eds) On building, defending and regulating the self: a psychological perspective. Psychology Press, pp 53–75

Hassabis D, Kumaran D, Maguire EA (2007) Using imagination to understand the neural basis of episodic memory. J Neurosci 27(52):14365–14374

Hazlitt W (1805) An essay on the principles of human action, privately published, London. https://books.google.co.uk/books?id=B2MAAAAAMAAJ&printsec=frontcover&source=gbs_ge_summary_r&cad=0#v=onepage&q&f=false. Accessed 14 Oct 2018

Kaski D (2002) Revision: Is visual perception a requisite for visual imagery? Perception 31(6):717–731

Hennessey BA (2010) The creativity-motivation connection. The Cambridge handbook of creativity 342–365

Iacoboni M (2005) Neural mechanisms of imitation. Curr Opin Neurobiol 15:632–637

Iacoboni M, Woods RP, Brass M, Bekkering H, Mazziotta JC, Rizzolatti G (1999) Cortical mechanisms of human imitation. Science 286(5449):2526–2528

Ingvar DH (1985) 'Memory of the future': an essay on the temporal organization of conscious awareness. Hum Neurobiol 4:127–136

Ingvar DH (1974) Patterns of brain activity revealed by measurements of regional cerebral blood flow. Alfred Benzon Symposium VIII, Copenhagen

Ingvar DH (1979) "Hyperfrontal" distribution of the cerebral grey matter flow in resting wakefulness: on the functional anatomy of the conscious state. Acta Neurol Scand 60:12–25

James W (1890/1950) The principles of psychology. Dover Publications, New York

Kaag J (2014) Thinking through the imagination: aesthetics in human cognition. OUP

Keysers C, Gazzola V (2010) Social neuroscience: mirror neurons recorded in humans. Curr Biol 20(8):R353–R354

Kozulin A (1998) Psychological tools: a sociocultural approach to education. Harvard University Press, Cambridge, MA

Levine B, Svoboda E, Hay JF, Winocur G, Moscovitch M (2002) Aging and autobiographical memory: dissociating episodic from semantic retrieval. Psychology and aging 17(4):677

Lord AB (1960/1991) The Singer of Tales. Harvard University Press, Cambridge, MA

Mancuso JC (1986) The acquisition and use of narrative grammar structure. In: Sarbin TR (ed) Narrative psychology: the stories nature of human conduct. Praeger, New York, pp 91–110

McVay JC, Kane MJ (2010) Adrift in the stream of thought: the effects of mind wandering on executive control and working memory capacity. Handbook of individual differences in cognition. Springer, New York, NY, pp 321–334

Meyza KZ, Knapska E (eds) (2018) Neuronal correlates of empathy: from rodent to human. Academic Press, San Diego

Miller GA (1956) The magical number seven, plus or minus two: Some limits on our capacity for processing information. Psychol Rev 63(2):81–97

Mithen SJ (1996) The prehistory of the mind a search for the origins of art, religion and science

Mooneyham BW, Schooler JW (2013) The costs and benefits of mind-wandering: a review. Can J Exp Psychol 67(1):11–18

Nunn P (2018) The edge of memory. Bloomsbury Sigma, London

Pace-Schott EF (2013) Dreaming as a story-telling instinct. Front Psychol 4:159

Pelaprat E, Cole M (2011) Minding the gap: imagination, creativity, and human cognition. Integr Psychol Behav Sci 45:397–418. Springer

Peirce CS (2002) Septième conference. Le pragmatisme comme logique de l'abduction. Charles Sanders Peirce. Pragmatisme et pragmaticisme. Oeuvres I., Paris: Les Éditions du Cerf 417–441

Praszkier R (2016) Empathy, mirror neurons and SYNC. Mind Soc 15(1):1–25

Premack DG, Woodruff G (1978) Does the chimpanzee have a theory of mind? Behav Brain Sci 1(4):515–526

Raichle ME, MacLeod AM, Snyder AZ, Powers WJ, Gusnard DA, Shulman GL (2001) A default mode of brain function. Proc Natl Acad Sci 98(2):676–682

Ramachandran VS, Hirstein W (1999) The Science of Art: a neurological theory of aesthetic experience. J Conscious Stud 6(6–7):15–51

Ratcliffe M (2006) Folk psychology is not folk psychology. Phenomenol Cogn Sci 5(1):31–52

Ratner C (2000) Agency and culture. J Theory Soc Behav 30:413–434

Rizzolatti G, Sinigaglia C (2007) Mirror neurons and motor intentionality. Funct Neurol 22(4):205

Schacter DL, Addis DR, Buckner RL (2007) Remembering the past to imagine the future: the prospective brain. Nat Rev Neurosci 8(9):657–661

Schacter DL, Addis DR, Hassabis D, Martin VC, Spreng RN, Szpunar KK (2012) The future of memory: remembering, imagining, and the brain. Neuron 76(4):677–694

Schacter DL, Gaesser B, Addis DR (2013) Remembering the past and imagining the future in the elderly. Gerontology 59(2):143–151

Schank R, Abelson RP (1995) Knowledge and memory: the real story, In Advances in Social Cognition, vol VIII. Erlbaum Associates, Lawrence

Schippers MB, Roebroeck A, Renken R, Nanetti L, Keysers C (2010) Mapping the information flow from one brain to another during gestural communication. Proc Natl Acad Sci 107(20):9388–9393

Schmajuk N, Aziz DR, Bates MJ (2009) Attentional–associative interactions in creativity. Creat Res J 21(1):92–103

Schutte NS, Stilinović EJ (2017) Facilitating empathy through virtual reality. Motiv Emot 41(6):708–712

Searle JR (1975) The logical status of fictional discourse. New Lit Hist 6(2):319–332

Shin D (2018) Empathy and embodied experience in virtual environment: to what extent can virtual reality stimulate empathy and embodied experience? Comput Hum Behav 78:64–73

Soteriou M (2018) The past made present: mental time travel in episodic recollection. In: New directions in the philosophy of memory. Routledge, pp 294–312

Stern A (1997) Virtual Babyz: believable agents with narrative intelligence. In: Mateas M, Sengers P (eds) Narrative intelligence. John Benjamins, Amsterdam

Sternberg RJ, Lubart TI (1999) The concept of creativity: prospects and paradigms. Handbook of creativity 1:3–15

Suddendorf T, Corballis MC (1997) Mental time travel and the evolution of the human mind. Genet
   Soc Gen Psychol Monogr 123:133–167
Suddendorf T, Corballis MC (2007) The evolution of foresight: what is mental time travel and is it
   unique to humans. Behav Brain Sci 30:299–351
Suddendorf T, Addis DR, Corballis MC (2009) Mental time travel and the shaping of the human
   mind. Philos Trans R Soc B Biol Sci 364(1521):1317–1324
Suddendorf T, Addis DR, Corballis MC (2011) Mental time travel and shaping of the human mind.
   In: Bar M (ed) Predictions in the brain: using our past to generate a future. OUP, New York, NY,
   pp 344–354
Tulving E (1972) Episodic memory. In: Tulving, Donaldson (eds) Organization of memory.
   Academic Press, New York
Tulving E (1984) Précis of elements of episodic memory. Behav Brain Sci 7:223–268
Tulving E (2002a) Chronesthesia: conscious awareness of subjective time. In: Principles of frontal
   lobe
Tulving E (2002b) Episodic memory: from mind to brain. Annu Rev Psychol 53(1):1–25
Vygotsky LS (1991) Imagination and creativity in the adolescent (trans. F. Smolucha). Sov Psychol
   29(1). (Original work 1931)
Wearing D (2005) Forever today: a memoir of love and amnesia. Random House
Wellman H (1990) The child's theory of mind. MIT Press, Cambridge, MA
Williamson T (2017) Semantic paradoxes and abductive methodology. Reflections on the Liar
   325–346
Whiten (1991) Natural theories of mind. Basil Blackwell, Oxford
Wollheim R (1984) The thread of life. Cambridge University Press, Cambridge
Ye Q, Song X, Zhang Y, Wang Q (2014) Children's mental time travel during mind wandering.
   Front Psychol 5:927

Chapter 3
Imagination and Design

Chapter Thumbnail

The central thesis of this book is that imagination is important to HCI and where better to begin this discussion than with the design of a digital artefact? When we design a new piece of technology (or engage in any design-related activity) there is an expectation that our imaginations will be at hand to generate ideas with respect to what the technology will do, and how it will look and how it will be experienced. This is imagination as mental time travel and creativity; and imagination as storytelling and as facilitating of social interaction. Having set ourselves what is a very broad target—the design process in all its stripes, and all four aspects of imagination, we will narrow our focus on how we use things ("design tools") to crystallize our imaginations.

Thus, the topic of this chapter may be characterised as variations on "thinking with things".

Firstly, consistent with current cognitive science (e.g. Clark 1998), we don't just think with our brains as we routinely employ with all kinds of external representations and artefacts. These different forms of "thinking with things" have been, in turn, studied in a variety of ways, for example, through the use of props in make-believe. This is the major theme of not only this chapter but also for Chap. 4. Instead of (say) toys, imagine thinking with sketches and prototypes.

Secondly, there is also evidence from the study of external cognition (Scaife and Rogers 1996) which is the "interaction between internal and external representations when performing cognitive tasks". In general, they describe external cognition as a form of computational offloading, which is the extent to which external representations can reduce the amount of cognitive effort required to solve a problem or complete a task. Here we are specifically concerned with capturing our imaginations with the use of sketches, external representations and then thinking with these. In each of these instances we will see how something (whether it be psychological, material or cultural—or a mixture) serves to make or help make material what we imagine.

© Springer Nature Switzerland AG 2020
P. Turner, *Imagination + Technology*, Human–Computer Interaction Series,
https://doi.org/10.1007/978-3-030-37348-1_3

3.1 Introduction

Imagination is the reflexive skill we use to explore and analyse the over-whelming number of ideas that are possible in every design situation. By imagination, we can visualize future compositions and explore the consequences of bringing a particular into existence

Nelson and Stolterman (2003a, b, p. 179)

There is abundant research which suggests that designers of all kinds employ a wide variety of different forms of thinking, for example, Nelson and Stolterman (2003a, b, p. 124) write, "Design draws on rational thinking, but is not merely a rationalized, logical process. It is a process that includes imagination, intuition, feeling and emotion as well." So, designers, it is fair to say, engage in creative thinking; and what might be described as productive thinking; analytical thinking; deductive thinking; inductive thinking; abductive thinking, problem-solving thinking and (heaven help us) "out-of-the-box" thinking but as ever there is only scant mention of imagination (see Lawson's *How designers think*, 2006). And this is doubly surprising as we all delight in imaginative design. Mithen (2001) has also observed that imagination is generally seen to be a desirable property of designs, "solutions", artistic works and, of course, people. While describing any of these as unimaginative would be regarded as pejorative and even insulting. This diversity and ubiquity, as we have already seen, has a downside in that imagination tends to be squeezed into catch-all terms like "creative thought" but this is clearly an unfair and incomplete assessment. Indeed, it might be argued that these definitions are unnecessary because we all have an intuitive understanding of imagination. While space precludes a detailed examination of this, a couple of vignettes provides a little flavour of design + imagination in the wild (or workshop), for example, the American inventor Thomas Edison was said to "sit at one of the lab tables, chew on a wad of tobacco, and make a little drawing of a new component. He'd ponder it, pass it around among his staff, and wander off to read a couple of technical manuals. He would frown … and commence to cogitate. He played with his stuff with the grace and zest of an artist, or child." Here we explicitly see Edison using sketches, manuals and the contributions and comments of his co-workers with a "playful" demeanour. So, Edison the inventor was creative, social, playful and relied on what is recognisably distributed cognition with its involvement with other minds (cognitions) and external representations.

Similarly, the industrial designer, Dreyfuss (1955) wrote of his practice as, "We [the designers] enter into close cooperation with engineers … we go over countless rough sketches. Components are arranged and re-arranged, working drawings and blueprints are made, some by the client's engineer, some by us, and frequently exchanged". Here the emphasis appears to be on distributed cognition and the propagation of the design across numerous artefacts and representations in a lively mixture of people and *countless* sketches. And finally, the English physicist Michael Faraday (1791–1867) who demonstrated the first electric generator, and electric motor, imagined electrical and magnetic fields as "lines of force" which may have been inspired by him watching the movement of flames in a wood fire. Thus, Faraday appears to have drawn a parallel between flickering flames and the imagined movement of magnetic flux. We can see from these three vignettes that our imaginations in action are distributed, embodied and embedded across different forms of representations including our use of language, signs and symbols, our bodies and gestures, other people and so forth.

The imaginative use of the external

Imagination is thus not confined to the brain and like cognition as a whole, it can be treated as distributed as well as embedded in our technological culture. So, we now consider how it has been examined.

We begin with Donald (1991, 1993) who has proposed a theory of human cognitive evolution drawing upon a range of evidence. He argues that in the last two million years we have experienced three cognitive transitions each of which has changed the ways in which we represent external reality and which, in turn, has enabled new forms of culture. These are described as mimetic skill, language and external symbols. He writes that each of these systems is based on an *inventive* capacity (his italics) and the products of these capacities including languages, systems, gestures, social ritual and images continue to be invented. Here he identifies *imagination* as an example of mimesis. He also offers the term *exogram*, based the idea of a memory engram, to refer to the use of external symbols. He notes that exograms last longer than human memories and have (potentially) a much greater capacity, and that they are easily transmitted, retrieved and manipulated by means of digital technology than their biological equivalents (1991, pp. 315–316). The use of exograms is important because they extend and support our cognitive abilities (including our imaginations) unlike any other creature which is restricted to engrams alone.

Next, in amongst the proposals for different forms of cognition, (e.g. distributed, embodied, extended, and so forth), is the work of Scaife and Rogers on external cognition. Their interest began with how we think with graphical and other forms of external representation, for example, beginning with graphs which allow us to re-present data but in a manner which renders them more comprehensible. And where better to see an example of this than the Crimean War of the 19th century. Florence Nightingale was a reforming nurse who used graphs to communicate the extent of casualties of the war. At that time the British were incurring significantly more casualties from disease such as cholera, typhus and poor medical treatment than from enemy action. Although these data were readily available they were not easily understood particularly by the decision-making classes of that time. Her pie-charts (see Fig. 3.1) changed their understanding and facilitated mutual understanding.

Finally, Scaiffe and Rogers also identified *graphical constraining* which refers to the kinds of inferences that can be made about the represented world from, say a particular form of a graph. Here the idea is that the relations between graphical elements in a representation are able to map onto the relations between the features of a problem space in such a way that they restrict (or enforce) the kinds of interpretations.

Finally, we briefly consider the work of Kirsh (1996, 2010) who has investigated why people create external representations to help them make sense of situations, instructions and to help with problem solving. He found that these representations save on cognitive resources but suggests that this explanation is not enough in itself.

Fig. 3.1 Nightingale's
military casualty statistics
(public domain)

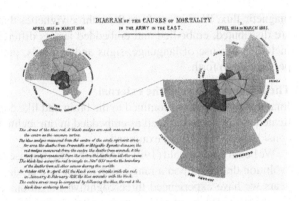

He goes on to argue that external representations enhance cognitive power and permit us to think the "unthinkable". His position rests on a novel treatment of the usefulness of the external. He begins by reminding us that people interact with and create external structures when thinking because through such interaction it is easier, more efficient and more effective than by working inside the head alone. He defines efficiency (i.e. speed, accuracy, fewer errors or greater speed) and effectiveness (coping with more demanding problems). He continues, "why bother to mark, gesture, point, mutter, manipulate inert representation, write notes, annotate, rearrange things, and so on? Why not just sit still and 'think'?"

In short, these other ways of thinking about external cognition change the domain and available range of cognitive operators. Kirsh writes that "as our environments and technology change, we will be able to think about things that today are unthinkable". There is a further reason why people interact with external representations: to prepare themselves to coordinate the internal and external components of cognition. We recall that Scaife and Rogers spoke of these processes as being interwoven and here the idea is developed further. This is both interesting and surprisingly commonplace, for example, before people use a map to way-find, they typically orient the map with their surroundings; they line the maps up with the world/shopping mall. Interestingly, mobile phones and tablet computers now come equipped with digital compasses and gyroscopes to help with this registration. He also notes from a series of studies that people were found to engage in "interpreting" actions when they follow, say, origami instructions. People were found to re-orient or register the origami paper with the instruction sheet; they were observed to self-talk, gesture, and move the paper about. These activities are part of making sense of the instructions. So, there is prima facie evidence that this kind of internal/external interweaving is likely to be true of imagination too and although this is a significantly under-researched domain, there are enough indications to suppose that imagination is not confined to our heads.

3.2 How We Make-Believe with Things

Making-believe is what children do when they pretend play (e.g. Harris 1998) and what game-players are doing when they are playing video-games (e.g. Granic et al. 2014) and, of course, what actors do on the stage (e.g. Goldstein and Bloom 2011). And on this basis, make-believe seems pretty much irrelevant to the serious business of designing digital technology. So, unsurprisingly, making-believe, despite being a rich and interesting domain, has not received much in the way of academic attention outside of children's psychological development, which has prompted us to offer our own definition which we have created from a cognitive scientific perspective.

We propose that make-believe comprises three components, namely, pretending, the use of props and cognitively decoupling (see Turner and Harviainen's, *Digital Make-Believe*, 2016). As we have said, pretending is usually treated as child's play, and is widely recognised that it is important to their social and cognitive development. Russ (2004), for example, has argued that the development of a number of cognitive and affective processes relies on pretend play, which he tells us involves the exercise of alternating cycles of divergent and convergent thinking, that is, the abilities to generate a variety of different ideas, story themes, and so forth and to weave them together. Pretend play also facilitates the expression of both positive and negative feelings, and the ability to integrate emotion with reason (e.g. Jent et al. 2011; Seja and Russ 1999). Early pretend play has also been implicated in creativity in later life (e.g. Russ 2004; Singer and Singer 2005). Further, when children assume different roles it allows them the opportunity to acquire social skills such as communication, problem solving, and empathy (Hughes 1999). We argue that all make-believe relies on pretending. Every child can pretend and this ability appears early in her development typically soon after their first birthday and this is very much earlier than the full maturation of their cognition (Leslie 1987). No matter, pretending is essential, if a little mysterious and has many of the characteristics—as we shall see—more loosely attributed to imagination.

Despite continuing to pretend throughout our adult lives it carries with it the suspicion that to pretend is to be dishonest or to dissemble or mislead and is associated with seeking to deceive. It also carries with it the association with playing, so much so that pretending and playing are often treated as near synonyms. This blurring offers useful insights into the nature of pretending, as it has been described as the "voluntary transformation of the here and now, the you and me, and the this or that, along with any potential action that these components of a situation might have", Garvey (1990). Whereas Rutherford et al. (2007, p. 1025) describe pretend play a little more directly as "acting as if something is when it is not", so we can treat pretending is "acting as-if".

This emphasis on acting or behaving also serves to identify pretending as an expression of our embodied cognition and as such pretending is both enabled and constrained by the capabilities and restrictions of our bodies. These aspects of pretending continue to be neglected by mainstream accounts of developmental psychology. In all, we treat pretending as the behavioural expression of imagination.

Fig. 3.2 Make-believing a banana is an (old style) telephone. Image by Peter McCarthy, licensed under CC BY-ND 2.0

For our second component of make-believe what we propose involves "thinking with things". Here we have in mind, thinking with props which serves to create fictional worlds which in turn are both defined and constrained by the props themselves (e.g. thinking with this "ray gun" transports me to a fictional world of space travel and space battles). Props can range from the natural to the artefactual and may offer any range of affordances or conventions which define their use—either real or imagined.[1] For example, a long wooden stick becomes a (hobby) horse; a banana becomes a telephone; shaping your hand in a particular way creates a gun or a "ray-gun". A banana is a nice example as it offers some of the affordances of an old-style telephone complete with an external "earpiece" and a "mouthpiece" (see Fig. 3.2).

Such props also show how they can be used as simple mock-ups or prototypes for digital systems. These make-believe artefacts also frequently embody cultural or conventional or copy-right dimensions too, for example, as a phaser, which is a product of the Star Trek® universe and cannot be used by someone pretending to be a Star Wars character armed with a light sabre. However, these constraints are not limited to play—as we have already seen in Scaife and Rogers's observations about graphical constraints. Toon (2010) in his *Models as Make-Believe* has identified their role in scientific reasoning arguing that scientific models "prescribe specific imaginings" that is, they afford and constrain particular kinds of reasoning directly analogous to the ways in which dolls, teddy bears and ray-guns prescribe the pretend play of children.

---

[1] The Nintendo web site promoting its products including the Wii, tells us that "*nobody does it quite like Wii. With games that give you the feeling of playing your favorite sports activities, and adventures that put a sword in your hand like never before, your own body's movements are used to interact with the games in fun and delightful ways – thanks to the Wii Remote Plus controller in your hand. [. . .] It responds to motion and rotation for enhanced control as you swing, swipe, thrust, or turn the controller. With Wii Remote Plus, your gaming experience becomes more active and immersive than you ever thought possible*". (Nintendo 2014, online). All of these gaming scenarios are based on the technology's wonderful graphics, and sound and the player's make-believe. The Wii must take the credit for enabling seniors to make-believe they were playing sport in their retirement homes and day-centres.

The final element of make-believe is cognitive decoupling in which we make-believe that we separate ourselves from the everyday to engage with the fictional world. This is not just a matter of switching our attention as it requires the creation and maintenance of a fictional world too. This most certainly not a matter of a suspension of disbelief as it is a consequence of actively making-believe. This decoupling may manifest in several different ways and to different degrees. It may take the form of something like a momentary day-dream or it might immerse or transport us to a fictional world sufficiently to allow us to share in the adventures of a superhero in the latest cinematic blockbuster. This decoupling liberates us from the here-and-now to enable us to explore and engage with the possible.

So, equipped, it might seem that we can imagine, or make-believe anything but, in practice there are limits and when these are breached, whatever we are participating in becomes unbelievable. For example, while watching a movie, encountering unbelievability might be experienced as a "plot hole" (e.g. Garau et al. 2004).

3.3 Not Playing Exactly

While we do not suggest that designing technology is just a matter of people playing with their set of design props, we do recognise that the underlying processes are congruent with the childhood forms. As we will see, a wide variety of props are available to prompt, suggest, constrain, direct and even afford design thinking. The props may act as what Darke (1979) calls a "primary generator" or as "design seeds".

Ryan (2008) applies a similar premise in her analysis of interactive digital fictional worlds, observing that such media rely on an "act of make-believe whose prototype can be found in children's role-playing games", which may take the form of first-person embodiment or third person observation. Make-believe has a major but unrecognised role in design where, for example, three-dimensional models of a proposed town enable architects, town planners and their clients to walk through them, and to explore and the make-believe buildings therein. Similarly, interaction designers use scenarios and prototypes to explore imaginary situations which they can populate with people (personas) to animate them. and within HCI as a whole as it is commonplace for users to be asked to evaluate a design by pretending to undertake make-believe tasks using a simple prototype.

We now consider the role of things in design thinking in HCI beginning with what is arguably the most famous of all design props namely *cultural probes* before briefly considering examples including design methods cards, sketching, and trajectories.

Cultural probes
Cultural probes (Gaver et al. 1999) were originally packages of maps, postcards, disposable cameras (this research pre-dated the wide availability of smart phones) and other materials designed to provoke inspirational responses from people who were involved in the design process (as pictured in Fig. 3.3). The idea was that the citizen designers photographed things which capture their attention or piqued their

Fig. 3.3 Cultural probe bag
and probe activity contents
designed to capture
conceptualisations of 'home'
© William Odom and
Doenja Oogjes

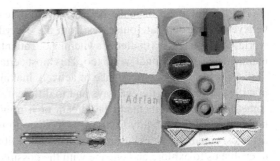

imagination while engaged in their everyday activities. As Gaver makes clear, "… we were after 'inspirational data' with the probes, to stimulate our imaginations rather than define a set of problems. We weren't trying to reach an objective view of … needs through the probes, but instead a more impressionistic account of their beliefs and desires, their aesthetic preferences and cultural concerns".

The first use of these probes was in what were described as "diverse communities", in that they were given to these older people to return fragmentary data (a photograph here, a postcard there and a diary entry whenever) over time. The probes were part of a strategy of pursuing understanding of the local cultures so that new designs wouldn't seem irrelevant or arrogantly imposed on the locals. The probes were distributed among groups of older people in three communities in: Majorstua, Oslo; Bijlmer, near Amsterdam; and Peccioli, near Pisa. They were intended to be aesthetically inviting and "delightful, but not childish or condescending" to encourage an informal attitude from participants.

So, did they work? Yes, the collage of disparate information returned by the participants did provoke imaginative design decisions but like all ethnographically collected or elicited data they are difficult to analyse because of their unique, subjective and embedded character. But as Gaver et al. (2004) noted, the probes were also appropriated by "other industrial and academic research and design groups" (p. 53). Gaver and his team observed that, "the problem is there has been a strong temptation to rationalize the Probes. People seem unsatisfied with the playful, subjective imaginative approach embodied by the original Probes, and so designed theirs to ask specific questions and produce comprehensible results, even use them to produce requirements analyses". The original probe may have been too imaginative to be useful for a solution and design focussed problem solving.

Design cards
Figure 3.4 illustrates another celebrated prop or props which are the IDEO methods cards (Stout 2003) which consist of a deck of 51 cards, each showing a different design method and an associated story or picture. These were designed to inspire creativity by inviting designers to try out and develop different approaches when designing. They were also, it turns out, the inspiration for the creation of many other sets of such cards. The Ideo cards are grouped into four categories, namely, *learn*, *look*, *ask* and *try*. The learn category, for example, is concerned with analysing data already

Fig. 3.4 A selection of IDEO cards

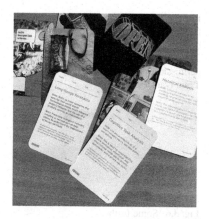

collected to identify patterns and bright ideas. And for each of these categories there are a set of techniques which might prove relevant, so again, under *learn* there are instructions on how to construct an affinity diagram and how to perform a cognitive task analysis and how to conduct a comparative product survey and so forth.

Since the appearance of these original cards, other researchers have developed their own, for example, the Personal Cardset (Sleeswijk et al. 2004) which can be used to help communicate the results of design sessions to designers. And Lucero and Arrasvuori (2010) have reported on their PLEX Cards which share some aspects with the other methods cards but were developed specifically to help facilitate playful interaction and to provide "a rich source of inspiration for creative processes". Finally, the aptly named *Inspiration cards* (Halskov and Dalsgård 2006) have been claimed to successfully frame and guide interaction design workshops.

Wölfel and Merritt (2013) have attempted to answer the question of these cards "do they work?" and to this end have examined and classified 18 different card systems. Their interest was in how comprehensive the coverage of the design space is and they concluded that while it was good it was not complete, and invited further work. Unhappily, they reported was no mention of quantity or quality of the additional imaginative ideas or concepts which such cards prompted.

Playful triggers

Playful triggers (Loi 2007) are tools which were also derived from Gaver's cultural probes but specifically build upon the notion of anomalous objects and odd experiences. All of the probes, trigger, highlight, and afford responses and experiences in their users and thereby enhancing our understand people's everyday lives. Playful Triggers are thus an informal, creative and playful tool that helps people re-enact and capture the interactions, conversations and relationships. Playful triggers are about getting at the blurred boundaries and the non-goal states which is another way of saying "playful".

Akama and Ivanka (2010) have reported on the use of playful triggers in working on a project into raising bushfire risk awareness (Figs. 3.5 and 3.6). The researchers write that they proved to be helpful in providing information about how space and

Fig. 3.5 Playful triggers for facilitating participatory design (Akama and Ivnaka 2010), images by kind permission Yoko Akama and Tania Ivanka

Fig. 3.6 Some further examples of examples of playful triggers

people interact and were able to create a dialogue between the 'inhabitants' of a specific context enabling relationships that could foster and sustain co-operative practices.

Finally, Yilmaz and colleagues (2016) have reported on the evidence for the use of design heuristics (which we again treat as props) during ideation. They identified 3457 concepts created by industrial and engineering designers across four different studies, from these a master set of 77 design heuristics is extracted from a variety of design problems and designers. The observed design heuristics capture ways to introduce variations into candidate concepts. Design heuristics can help designers explore alternative concepts in early conceptual design. Example heuristics for idea generation and their application from Yilmaz et al. 2016, with permission from Elsevier (Figs. 3.7 and 3.8).

In reviewing the use of a number of different design props including probes, cards, triggers and heuristics we consistently found a disappointing lack of evidence of anyone writing of imagination, make-believe or any permutation such as "creative imagination". The use of these props seemed to be a matter of simple pragmatism, using them because they worked but don't worry about how or why.

However, nor was there any evidence of the usefulness of the props being evaluated either qualitatively (of the form, "we managed to brainstorm 50% more ideas when we used the cards …") or qualitatively ("the team found the cards broke the ice more effectively than the usual sitting around looking at each other").

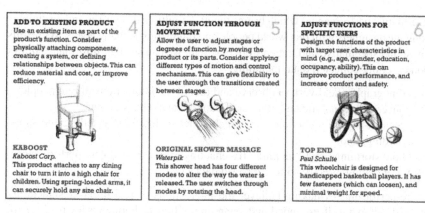

Fig. 3.7 Sample design heuristics with examples of their application. From Yilmaz et al. 2016, with permission from Elsevier

Fig. 3.8 A concept for a backpack-based solar oven using an *Attach product to user* heuristic, combined with an *Add functions* heuristic. From Yilmaz et al. 2016, with permission from Elsevier

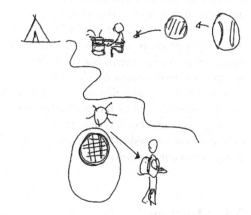

Bodystorming

Bodystorming may be thought of as form of "prototyping in context" or as acting as-if with whatever is ready-to-hand. Jones (2013) tells us that "It allows the team and stakeholders to experience some of the functions and working relationships of proposals, either during their formation or after prototyping." Bodystorming is typically achieved by role-playing an interaction with fellow actors and props. This might be either improvisation, or achieved by immersing oneself in an environment similar to that being designed for. Bodystorming is an immersive ideation method for exploring ideas through role-playing and physical interaction with props, prototypes, actual products, and physical spaces. The goal of bodystorming is to understand the relationships between people, their physical location, and the stuff (e.g., tools, devices, materials) they use their.

The origins of bodystorming lie with Burns et al. (1994) who tell us that he and his colleagues, were inspired by Laurel's *Computers as Theatre* to develop "informance" (informative performance) which brings together multiple discourses and disciplines to engage designers with real world people and interaction at many levels. While this may sound speculative and not entirely practical, we can see that Informance draws upon carefully collected data, including:

(1) ethnographic fieldwork to observe and record the interactions of real people;
(2) conversation analytic and ethnomethodological analysis of data;
(3) scenario-based interaction design techniques including storytelling and story-boarding; and,
(4) "bodystorming" and "repping" (re-enacting everyday peoples' performances) for engaging directly with real world data.

By "re-performing" (making-believe) the interactions of real users, designers are able to develop a well-grounded understanding of how technologies are really used, and are able to imagine more effectively potential future uses of how their products.

Another bodystorming scenario suggested by Oulasvirta et al. (2003) involves role playing elderly users (with memory problems) as they try to remember product information in a supermarket or drug store.

Bodystorming has been applied to the design of mobile learning experiences and robotic products and most recently, Porfirio et al. (2019) have provide a very nice example of the use of bodystorming as a means to inform and support inter-disciplinary design teams which are creating complex ("social") human-robot inter-actions. They recognise that any one of their designers may not have the necessary formal understanding of human interactions with technology and the expertise to create a working robotic system so, to leverage the team's everyday understanding of interaction, they asked them to engage in "acting out" or "role-playing" how they expect a robot might behave.

3.4 Sketching

Suppose we are tasked with designing a website or an app (or something equally digital and interactive), what do we do in practice? We may reach for some design cards or, we would suggest that many arm themselves with a pencil and paper and begin to crystallise their imaginations. The result of this exercise is likely to be a sketch, not a drawing or prototype, but a sketch. Sketches suggest and explore rather than confirm and are …quick, timely, inexpensive, disposable, plentiful and ambiguous and "*Sketches […] are an aid to thinking and, we maintain, under certain circumstances, their making is thinking itself*" (Goldschmidt (2003).

Sketching, as part of the design process, is important but for two reasons in particular. Firstly, imagination connects to a rough outline on paper as, in some sense, they are both "visual"; secondly, sketching is widely recognised to scaffold and stimulate thinking (and in certain quarters is treated as almost a form of "thinking" in its own right). Indeed, Fallman (2003) writes that sketching is often thought of as simply a way to externalise 'images' from the mind of the designer. Sketching then becomes a useful way in which artefacts that are as yet intangible may be transferred from the designer's mind to (say) paper. From this perspective, sketching serves the designer to express themselves while communicating within the stakeholder group. So, there is more to sketches than just about communicating early design ideas.

Goldschmidt (2003) also notes that these incomplete, spontaneously drawings we call sketches were called "pensieri," meaning "thoughts" in Italian. Sketches were then, and still are today, an aid to thinking and, we maintain, under certain circumstances, their making is thinking itself (that is, it is embedded, embodied cognition). Goldschmidt (2003) tells us that sketching has only a short history and may have originated in the late-fifteenth century in Europe and it is associated with the appearance of more-affordable paper being developed for printing. She tells us that artists were, for the first time, able to make study drawings, or "sketches". "This inventive process" is an iterative process of jotting down ideas in the form of language or graphic drawings and of modifying them, re-evaluating them, editing them, and so on, to transform or perfect an initial concept or solution. A nice example of this is the Philippe Starck's Juicy Salif lemon squeezer which a highly desirable kitchen ornament (and the original sketch of which upon a soiled table napkin is now in the Alessi Museum. It depicts the very first sketches of what would become the iconic lemon squeezer). Thus, a sketch balances a minimal amount of detail with a sufficient degree of refinement.

Designers sketch to capture on paper their first impressions of what the design might look like; and they then use this to redefine, improve, embellish, or reject these first drafts of their imagination. This process helps the designer to find unexpected consequences, is what Goldschmidt (1991) refers to as the 'dialectics of sketching' which comprise a dialogue between 'seeing that' and 'seeing as'. In many ways a sketch forms the ideal bridge between design and imagination. While Suwa et al. (1998) suggest that sketching serves a number of purposes the first is as an external memory device (and as such may be as a prop).

3.5 Designing with Stories

We return to our discussion of make-believe and pose a simple question –what is it for? We identify two related purposes for pretending, and while this list is not exhaustive, it is reassuringly broad. Firstly, for children, pretending (as pretend play) has an important role in "bootstrapping" our social, affective and cognitive development, and secondly pretending enables us to create stories by which we explore and access the world. We introduced storytelling as the third of the farthings in Sect. 2.4 but we now focus on storytelling with respect to design.

By way of a brief reprise, we recognise pretending as being foundational to our ability to engage with stories. Following the commentary on Searle (1979) in Schaeffer (2013), we adopt Searle's premise that fictional narratives—stories—firstly comprise pretend speech acts in which the author is pretending to assert that events of the story took place. Secondly, for Searle, stories are episodes of "intended play-ful pretense" where the act of pretending is shared between reader and author and narratives "publicly function as props in a game of make-believe". Although the nature and operation of fictional logic is deeply contested in philosophy and literary theory (and is beyond our scope here), most accounts of the nature of fiction and "truth in fiction" argue for the role of pretence and make-believe (inter alia, Lewis 1983; Currie 1990; Byrne 1993; Goodman 2011; Gatzia and Sotnak 2013). Byrne (1993), for instance, argues that authors invite readers to "make believe that certain propositions are true" following the case made in Currie's work, which asserts that "the author who produces a work of fiction is engaged in a communicative act, an act that involves having a certain kind of intention: the intention that the audience shall make believe the content of the story that is told" (Currie 1990, p. 24). Ryan (2008) applies such premises in her analysis of interactive digital fictional worlds, observing that such media rely on an "act of make believe whose prototype can be found in children's role-playing games", which may take the form of first-person embodiment or third person observation.

Scenarios, personas, user stories, and so forth represent only a small number of the very many ways we have created stories to help design digital, interactive technology. These are all quite different but have at least one characteristic in common, namely, they are broadly story-based.

Story-based design

A scenario is a little story which places at the centre of its narrative, the technology (or a digital service, or this or that which is to be designed or evaluated). The scenario tends to be simply textual or it may be more like a strip cartoon in which case it is usually described as a storyboard. Scenarios, almost by default, are written in plain language as they are intended to be understood by specialist and non-specialist alike. However, Howard et al. (2002) and Svanæs and Seland (2004) are among a number who regard scenarios as something which can be "acted out" by third-party actors or role-playing users. In addition to taking a number of forms, scenarios have alternate names such as user stories (e.g. Cohn 2004) or use cases (Alexander and Maiden 2004) depending on their origins or how they are being used. Figure 3.9 provides a scenario, a title and a sense of the tone "Jim can't sleep: its amazing anyone sleeps round here", a photograph suggesting a medical scene and Jim appears to be a young man, and a sketch of the context (a hospital ward).

Scenarios began to appear as a design tool in the 1980s (Young and Barnard 1987 is an early example), and their proper use became a matter of academic debate in the early 1990s, (e.g. Karat and Karat 1992) then they appeared as a fully formed design method in Carroll's *Scenario Based Design* (1995). The major development work on scenarios per se appears to have been completed about then and the following extracts are illustrative for work and home contexts.

(1) "Anna is 45 years old and a nurse. She works at the surgical ward, where she is manager during five years. One of her responsibilities as ward manager is performing the final authorization of all the invoices. She has just met the last patient for the day and has now time left for some paperwork before going home

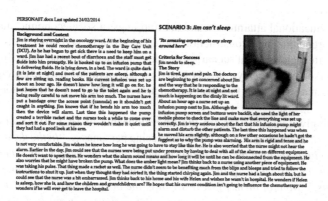

Background and Context

Jim is staying overnight in the oncology ward. At the beginning of his treatment he could receive chemotherapy in the Day Care Unit (DCU). As he has begun to get sick there is a need to keep him on a ward. Jim has had a recent bout of diarrhoea and the staff must get fluids into him promptly. He is hooked up to an infusion pump that is delivering fluids. He is lying down, in a bed. The ward is quite dark (it is late at night) and most of the patients are asleep, although a few are sitting up, reading books. His current infusion was set up about an hour ago. He doesn't know how long it will go on for, he just hopes that he doesn't need to go to the toilet again and he is being really careful to not move his arm too much. The nurses have put a bandage over the access point (cannula) so it shouldn't get caught in anything. Jim knows that if he bends his arm too much then the device will alarm. Last time this happened the pump created a terrible racket and the nurses took a while to come over and sort it out. For some reason they wouldn't make it quiet until they had had a good look at his arm.

SCENARIO 3: Jim can't sleep

"Its amazing anyone gets any sleep around here"

Criteria for Success
Jim needs to sleep.

The Story
Jim is tired, gaunt and pale. The doctors are beginning to get concerned about Jim and the way that he is responding to the chemotherapy. It is late at night and not much is happening on the dimly lit ward. About an hour ago a nurse set up an infusion pump next to Jim. Although the infusion pump screen and buttons were backlit, she used the light of her mobile phone to check the line and make sure that everything was set up correctly. Jim is very anxious about the fact that his infusion pump might alarm and disturb the other patients. The last time this happened was when he moved his arm slightly, although on a few other occasions he hadn't got the foggiest as to why the pump was alarming. His arm is rigid and tense and he is not very comfortable. Jim wishes he knew how long he was going to have to stay like this for. He is also worried that the nurse might not hear the alarm. Earlier in the day, Jim could see that the nurses were being put under pressure by having to deal with all of the alarms on different equipment. He doesn't want to upset them. He wonders what the alarm sound means and how long it will be until he can be disconnected from the equipment. He also worries that he might have broken the pump. What does the amber light mean? Jim thinks back to a nurse using another piece of equipment. He was taking his pulse. That thing made a racket as well. The nurse didn't seem to be benefiting much from the blips and bleeps and tried to follow the instructions to shut it up. Just when they thought they had sorted it, the thing started chirping again. Jim and the nurse had a laugh about this, but he could see that the nurse was a bit embarrassed. Jim thinks back to his home and his wife Helen and wishes he wasn't in hospital. He wonders if Helen is asleep, how she is, and how the children and grandchildren are? He hopes that his current condition isn't going to influence the chemotherapy and wonders if he will ever get to leave the hospital.

Page 12 of 19

Fig. 3.9 Scenario documenting real life use of an interactive medical device. From Vincent and Blandford (2015), licensed under CC BY 4.0

for the day…" [Scenario continues with Anna's interaction with the invoicing system.] (Johansson and Arvola 2007a, b)

(2) "Sixteen year old Becki is really excited. She's going to the Olympic Park Velodrome to see one of the cycling events with her two friends Alisha and Danielle. They get the over ground from Streatham, where Becki lives with her mum and step dad, to London Bridge where they hop on the tube to the Olympic Park. Twenty minutes later they get out at a very crowded Stratford tube station. As she's coming out of the tube, Becki's phone gets signal and she hears it beep…" [Scenario continues with more biographical detail as Becki reads the text message and the phone is snatched from her hand.] (Technology Strategy Board 2010)

As can be seen, these are little stories about technology with the people in them being little more than sketchy characters with a limited repertoire of traits. And with the exceptions of such ideas as *pastiche scenarios* (e.g. Blythe and Wright 2008; Blythe and Dearden 2008) which adapt well-known fictional characters from fiction, including Dickens' Scrooge, and television's Abe Simpson and Victor Meldrew (a popular BBC comedy character) to create lively, recognisable characters for designing with elderly people.

By the end of the last millennium this changed as ubiquitous technology, in the form of the smartphone, began to take on a greater importance and in that wake came the persona.

Persona-based design

Personas provide those well-rounded characters deemed to be missing from scenarios. Cooper (1999) intended putting a 'face on the users' by involving creating characters with multiple attributes and, personalities and histories. These character sketches are fictional (and hence make-believe), composite descriptions of people, complete with names, gender, age, occupations, friends, and potentially all of the attributes of real people including membership of an ethnic group, likes and dislikes, particular educational attainments and the trappings of socioeconomic status. Their advocates argue that their construction should be an early, perhaps even first, step in the design lifecycle and that scenarios should constructed around them. In Cooper's method, personas are always closely based on ethnographic user research. The use of personas may also help the designer engage with the people for whom they are designing.

Interestingly, Lene Nielsen (in the Encyclopaedia of HCI 2014) writes of the importance of exercising imagination while using personas ... *"In the design process, we begin to imagine how the product is to work and look before any sketch is made or any features described. If the design team members have a number of persona descriptions in front of them while designing, the personas will help them maintain the perspective of the users. The moment the designers begin to imagine how a possible product is to be used by a persona, ideas will emerge. Thus, I maintain that the actual purpose of the method is not the persona descriptions, but the ability to imagine the product. In the following, I designate these product ideas as scenarios. It is in scenarios that you can imagine how the product is going to work and be used, in what context it will be used, and the specific construction of the product. And it is during the work with developing scenarios that the product ideas emerge and are described. The persona descriptions are thus a means to develop specific and precise descriptions of products."*

Nielsen (2014) writes further that there are four different varieties of personas which she lists as goal-directed; role-based; her own which are "engaging"; and the final category which are fiction-based. She tells us that advocates of the first three agree that a persona should be based on data, while, the fiction-based perspective is a product of the "designers' intuition and assumptions". Scenarios, personae, storyboards, no matter what the trope, involve fictional worlds which, we would argue, are the products of—by definition—make-believe.

Storyboards

While storyboards can loosely be thought of as illustrated scenario, their origins lie with and filmic and animated media (Hart 1998), and share many of the characteristics of comic strips (Arvola and Artman 2007; Haesen et al 2010). As defined succinctly by Truong et al (2006) as a "short graphical description of a narrative", storyboards play a well-established role as props in the practice of interactive technology design. As Arvola and Artman (2007) point out, they are a form of model-making, where the model is a representation of what will happen in "the virtual world of hypothetical user activity where a future design solution will be used". Alongside the textual narrative of a scenario, they serve to stimulate, crystallise, communicate and document the designer's imagination, the level of detail depicted broadly increasing with the maturation of the design process.

Van der Lelie (2006) for example, notes the value of sketched storyboards early in design in supporting "visual thinking, which is vital to the creative process", just as in film their use allows directors to 'see' how a scene will unfold. At the end of a design project, though this is a rather less widespread practice, a fully realised storyboard may be employed to sell a finished product to a client. But it is the intermediate stages of design, where the storyboard acts as a resource for the communication of imagination, which are of most interest here.

Perhaps the most widely reported use of storyboards is in the sharing of an early design—necessarily an imaginary one, since the designed object does not yet exist—with its potential users and between co-designers. Figure 3.10 from Durrant et al. (2018) is a very typical instance. Here the storyboards, in the form of a "picture book" were used to stimulate discussion and reflection among stakeholders around digital technologies designed to support lifespan transitions.

In such cases, what is afoot is the fostering of what Truong et al. and van Der Lelie term 'empathy': in designers for potential users, in users themselves for others who will experience the future technologies, and between designers themselves for their differing design ideas. We would, of course, characterise such activity as the use of imagination in perspective taking. Moreover, as van der Lelie among others observes, storyboards serve as a vehicle for reflection on "visualised", i.e. imagined, interactions. This notion of a reflective conversation is amplified by Sirkin and Ju (2014), writing of the design of physically interactive technologies, who comment that designers' understanding builds through alternating the consideration of sketched storyboards and material prototypes. However, while the contribution of storyboards as discussed thus far is as a stimulus to design imagination, and often shared imagination, the technique also brings its own constraints. These range from the simple and practical limitations of skill in sketching (Truong et al. 2006), particularly for novice designers, to the rather more subtle tendency to restrict imagined

Fig. 3.10 Storyboards from *Charting the Digital Lifespan* picture book, to support reading and reflection in the context of discussion. Durrant et al. (2018), licensed under CC BY 4.0

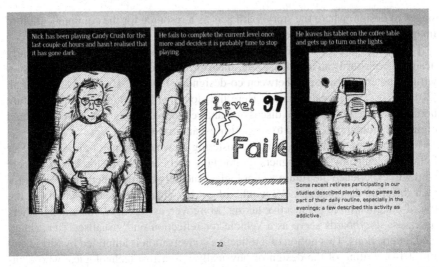

Some recent retirees participating in our studies described playing video games as part of their daily routine, especially in the evenings; a few described this activity as addictive.

Fig. 3.11 A detail from the Digital Lifespan picture book. Durrant et al. (2018), licensed under CC BY 4.0

further design alternatives to variants of those captured on the storyboard pages as these become ever more fully realised, and the problem noted by van der Lelie (2006) that the [imagined] experience of the 'readers' of storyboards is necessarily limited by individual prior experience and knowledge (Fig. 3.11).

Designing with trajectories

Trajectories (also known as the trajectories framework) have emerged as a means of creating complex mixed reality experiences (Benford et al. 2009). These experiences combine interactivity with live performance and exhibit complex and extended spatial and temporal structures which are organised around the metaphor of a journey. Some of these journeys have been captured in film, including Desert Rain (1999); Uncle Roy All Around You (2003); and Day of the Figurines (2006) to which the reader is directed.

A trajectory is a journey through a user's possible experiences of the technology, place, other people, different roles and a myriad of other possible elements. In some respects, trajectories, resemble the proposed structural elements of narratology, namely the text, the story, the *fabula* and the *syuzhet* (see for example, Bal 1997). The fabula refers to the underlying events and circumstances of which a given story is only one possible account. The *syuzhet* is "the way a story is organized" or the plot.

Despite the similarities, trajectories are a good deal more comprehensive and powerful as they offer multiple routes for multiple plays though the available experiences. Nonetheless, we treat the trajectories framework as an instance of storytelling rather than as a prop per se. Writing from the perspective of imagination, this is quite a feat of storytelling. The next three figures are from "Uncle Roy all around you" (2005).

Figure 3.12 is an illustration of a number of interleaved annotated trajectories

Fig. 3.12 Interleaved trajectories in the mixed reality game "Uncle Roy all around you", image by kind permission of Steve Benford

from the games. Figure 3.13 is an image from Uncle Roy showing a player eliciting and following directions in the real world. And Fig. 3.14 shows the player's location in a virtual map of the playing area.

Fig. 3.13 A player of the Uncle Roy mixed reality game

Fig. 3.14 A screenshot of the Uncle Roy mixed reality game Images from the mixed reality game "Uncle Roy all around you", by kind permission of Steve Benford

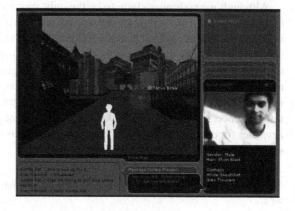

"Uncle Roy[2] all around you" is an example of urban gaming wherein a player is tasked with finding uncle Roy following clues and instructions fed to him or her by cell phone text messages. However, every time the player moves their position is communicated to other players (and their location appears on a map) who are trying to hunt him down. Meanwhile a small group of performance artists (called Blast Theory) also shadow the player interacting and manipulating him or her as they pursue uncle Roy.

More recently, in a survey of how trajectories have been used by the wider community, Velt et al. (2017) found that they have proved an effective and successful in four different ways:

a. As a sensitizing concept to inform future studies; and
b. As vehicles for compiling craft knowledge. By this the authors mean the process that embeds the practical knowledge of experience creators into the trajectories framework. This process remains open-ended as the design of experiences continues to evolve.
c. As a means by which requirements for future technologies can be identified and
d. A means of enabling the dramaturgy of interactive user experiences.

3.6 The Creative Use of Technology

Unless digital technology is used as intended (that is, it is a fairly close match to an underlying task structure), it has likely been appropriated. We appropriate technology by making it our own whenever we can. Even mass-produced personal computers are tweaked, personalised, decorated, configured and so forth to more closely match how we want to use them. More than this, appropriation often refers to the use of a tool of an unanticipated or in an unexpected manner. So, a common enough example is to use email for note keeping: we have an idea and compose an email to this effect and send it to ourselves. This is effective because email certainly was the daily focus of office life and an email is always available.

Although we no longer claim to be the only species that uses tools, the tools and technology we use are still intimately connected with defining who we are and where we came from. Heidegger tells us that the ontology of technology, that is, the meaning of technology as a mode of revealing, that is, the key quality of technology is its ability to disclose things. Part of his argument is etymological as he defines techné—the root of the word technology—means having the power to brings-something-forth into presence (Heidegger 1971). We adopt this insight as, brings-something [forth] into presence, seems very much like what we might mean by appropriation ("finding new uses for existing technology") and this also points to the technology itself as the source of this.

---

[2]https://www.nottingham.ac.uk/research/groups/mixedrealitylab/works/uncle-roy-all-around-you.aspx.

It is to art that we should look to find the best and most blatant examples of appropriation. Artists have always borrowed from each other, with Picasso famously observing that, "Good artists copy, great artists steal". Within the arts, appropriation involves the practice of taking something from one context and using as a kernel for creating another (Schneider 2003) and is considered an essential precondition of the artistic practice itself (Grew 2004). Here there are very many examples of this readily available providing we are happy to define the media as arts. For example, television series are constantly being re-imaged, re-invented together with ill-fitting prequels. Movies employ pastiche, homage and allusion or may simply poke fun. Many forms of art actively rely on appropriated elements. Art appropriates ideas, images, sound and styles from any and all aspects of natural and artefactual worlds. In essence, appropriation involves the creation or the opening of a new disclosive space. A disclosive space is an "organized set of practices for dealing with oneself, other people, and things that produces a relatively self-contained web of meanings" (Spinosa et al. 1997, p. 17). The term captures a very specific understanding of ourselves and of how we are in the world. Steampunk is an example of one such disclosive space (see Figs. 3.15 and 3.16). Figure 3.15 is an image of the Aide

Fig. 3.15 Aide Memoire, image by kind permission of Tom Flint

Fig. 3.16 Steampunk desktop A Steampunked desktop (use of image: Jake von Slatt 2007 licensed under CC BY-SA 2.0)

Memoire, a fully realised product constructed from discarded testing equipment. Born out of a series of creative sessions exploring the broad theme of interactivity the product was developed in partnership between Tom Flint and Tommy Dylan. The intention was to produce real tangible products with which people could have direct and personal interactions.

The work of Levine and his colleagues is often cited (e.g. Schneider 2003; Grew 2004; Falzone et al. 2011) in discussions of the appropriation of art where it is argued that adapting and re-purposing the world and artefacts around us is what constitutes "cultural discourse". A good example is Warhol's (1962) "Campbell's Soup" which comprises a series of canvases each with an image of a Campbell's soup can label. The origins of this piece, it is said, were prompted by his fondness for Campbell's soup and his ability to "see" the labels differently.

However, artistic appropriation is not confined to the atelier but can be found on the "street". Traceurs/traceuses (practitioners of Parkour) regularly disclose and appropriate fresh uses of existing structures and spaces (e.g. Childress 2004; Debord 1967). Traceurs claim that they develop what are known as "parkour eyes" (e.g. Ameel and Tani 2011) described as a "childlike perception of the space around them".

From these artistic perspectives, appropriation involves imagining the world differently ("seeing as") and then acting upon this accordingly. It is difficult not to be reminded of either Walton (1990) or Gibson (1977) at this point.

The appropriation of technology
The appropriation of digital technologies has received sustained attention from within the human-computer interaction communities though, to date, most of this interest has been in the results or products of appropriation, that is, the new uses to which the existing artefact is put.

The appropriation of digital technology is something of an umbrella term reflecting the heterogeneity of its origins. It is a hotchpotch of ideas includes customisation (e.g. MacLean et al. 1990), personalisation (e.g. Blom and Monk 2003), do-it-yourself design (e.g. Akah and Bardzell 2010), "mash-ups" (e.g. Zang et al. 2008) and so forth. Thus, these processes of "making technology our own" vary from the superficial to full blown personalisation which some researchers have gone so far as to call "ensoulment".

Domestication
Silverstone and Haddon (1996) coined the term "domestication" to describe appropriation as the way in which technologies are integrated and adapted into everyday life. They based this on the parallel they draw between with the domestication of wild animals as sources of food, clothing, work and protection and digital technology. Dourish (2003, p. 467) re-iterates this view by describing appropriation as, the way in which technologies are adopted, adapted and incorporated into working practice. He stresses the practical and situated aspects of appropriation writing that, *"Appropriation is the way in which technologies are adopted, adapted and incorporated into working practice. This might involve customization in the traditional sense (that is, the explicit reconfiguration of the technology in order to suit local needs)*

…". As ever, appropriation which is necessarily a creative practice does not mention imagination.

These sentiments have been echoed by Carroll (2004) who proposes that appropriation is an extended process occurring after the introduction of a technology and between the two states, "technology-as-designed" and "technology-in-use." Her model highlights the importance of actual use over projected or intended use. More recently, Belin and Prié (2012) have described the appropriation of digital technology in similar terms writing that it is the process by which people continuously integrate artefacts into their practices. This is appropriation as "design-in-use" (or artefact evolution) occurring in response to the demands of the situation users encounter.

Perhaps the most famous example of software détournement is "Untitled Game" which was created by the hacker group JODI which used the Quake game engine as a means to radically remix versions of the game (Yuill 2001). Thus, JODI appropriated Quake as a "work of art". Their concern was not to excise the original format but to replace sections of with abstract, though still playable forms. "Untitled Game" is thus a visualisation of the abstract, drawing on notions of modernist abstract painting, but utilising the materials of computer software and hardware rather than paint and canvas. The manufacturers opting for Open Source code made JODI's re-appropriation of Quake possible. This decision was largely driven by games manufacturers realising that amongst their audiences there are many hackers that like to 'mod' (modify) or 'patch' sections of code to their games. The 'naked' Lara Croft in Tomb Raider, being a famous example. Thus, games manufacturers realised that leaving these possibilities open for gamers to change left more room for the development of their games and the communities that surround them. Indeed, much of the software in the open source community evolves by the process of collective authorship among a worldwide development team. These types of détournement (re-routing or hijacking) go far beyond the game itself and become manifestations of something entirely different. They become manifestations of a critical engagement with the material of code itself, once again highlighting the spectacular nature of media relations and uncovering the sophistication of educated consumers that are prepared to go beyond the constraints they are confronted with produce commentary. So, this kind of appropriation is seen as a political or an artistic expression of the coder/player but sadly, not one which recognises the flowering of the technological imagination.

Making

Recent years has seen an exponential growth in making, and with it a recognition and interest from the academic HCI community. Bardzell et al. (2017) *HCI's Making Agendas* highlights this growing interest in making in the well-respected Foundations and Trends ® in Human-Computer Interaction series of books. The book paints a very attractive picture of personal empowerment, crowd-funding, the democratisation of computing and the move from endless mass production (and replacement) to repair, maintenance and re-use.

In his Shaping Things, Sterling (2005) suggested that we détourne the then burgeoning Internet of Things to become more fully aware of the ecological role of objects in the world. Sterling coins the neologism "Spimes" to refer to future objects that could be made aware of their context and transmit "cradle-to-grave" information about where they have been, where they are and where they are going. Jeremijenko's *How Stuff Is Made project* is a response to Sterling's theories, and comprises a visual encyclopaedia (wiki) of photo-essays produced by engineering and design students that document how objects are manufactured and investigating both the labour conditions of that manufacture and its environmental impact. She describes herself as a thingker (thing/thinker) which nicely recalls our discussion of thinking with things in Chap. 2.

Work is reported by Akah and Bardzell (2010) on the relationship between personal identity and the act of appropriating digital objects in the home—specifically 'do-it-yourself design'—to inform the design of empowering products. Using examples from the Steampunk movement they explore personal appropriation and the do-it-yourself (DIY) approach to design and sense of self. Steampunk is a genre of 'modern' science fiction set in Victorian times, examples include, Moore's the League of Extraordinary Gentlemen and Baxter's Anti Ice. For appropriation to occur the everyday designer must be open to interpretation as to the purpose, function, and interaction of the digital artefact. This individual appropriation occurs at home as there is little or no personal choice in most workplaces. This appropriation is about designing (re-designing) artefacts that are adaptable to the user, empowering and reflecting the user's personal identity. The authors redefine appropriation as the act of adapting an artefact to oneself in a way that not only redefines the artefact, but also relates the artefact to one's sense of self. They define personal identity as the unique set of experiences, qualities, characteristics, thoughts, behaviours, and so forth which recognisably define an individual or collection of individuals, and the relationships occurring between them.

Steampunk has been described as a revival of the 19th Century Arts and Crafts Movement with its emphasis of hand-crafting. The politics (or aesthetics) of Steampunk is a rejection of the 'always-connected', homogenized-commodities by creating things of value and meaning by drawing inspiration from the steam/Victorian age.

Accounts of appropriation
Appropriation has been described in term of design theory (e.g. Sengers and Gaver 2006), Activity theory (e.g. Bannon and Bødker 1991; Bødker and Klokmose 2012), different forms of structuration theory (e.g. Giddens 1984, Orlikowski 1992) and typically for the current discussion in terms of affordance, schemata and design life-cycles (e.g. Carroll 2004; DeSanctis and Poole 1994; Dix 2007; Salovaara 2008; Salovaara et al. 2011). However, there is no account of the imaginative use of technology in which imagination or make-believe feature. Perhaps the best known and most widely cited theoretical treatment of appropriation is the work of Salovaara (2008). His argument begins by observing that most of the work to date on appropriation has focused in its practical and practice aspects. He then claims that appropriation can be understood as being the result of interpretation (or re-interpretation) in which an individual perceives new opportunities for action (affordances) with the artefacts. In doing so they acquire a new mental usage schema. This schema holds both the new conceptual knowledge (that is, knowledge of the new uses to which the artefact

Fig. 3.17 Astronaut John L. Swigert, Jr., Apollo 13 Command Module Pilot, holds the "mailbox" a jerry-rigged arrangement which the Apollo 13 astronauts built to use the Command Module lithium hydroxide canisters to purge carbon dioxide from the Lunar Module (NASA 1970)

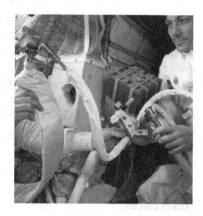

can be put) and the practical "know-how" allowing the individual to put the artefact to this new use. To achieve this, Salovaara proposes modifying Neisser's perceptual cycle. This cycle, also employs a schema to mediate and direct interaction with the world. In essence, Salovaara has argued that appropriation involves modifying both our conceptual and practical understanding of technology.

Now, let us contrast this with a real-life example. On April 14th 1970, the astronauts on board Apollo XIII while 180000 miles from earth, hear a "pretty large bang". The explosion saw the service module lose its liquid oxygen and for the crew to rely on the lunar module for breathable air. As the lunar module was only designed to support two men for a short time on the moon's surface, this left the three-man crew with an excess of carbon dioxide. Carbon dioxide is ordinarily regulated by way of chemical scrubbers which absorb it. Among the problems the crew faced was making the scrubbers on the lunar module work with those in the command module. One had "square" fittings, the other "round" fittings the challenge was to make one work with the other using only a small amount of stuff (props) including air hoses, cardboard covers, plastic bags and a sock (but that might just be in the movie version as I could find no mention of it in the official transcripts). This was not a matter of rejiggling conceptual models but applying creative imagination and seeing these props as something else. Figure 3.17 sees two of the astronauts constructing the "mailbox".

3.7   Conclusion

We have proposed that imagination and make-believe do not just contribute some kind of intangible "creativity" to the design process but are central to how ideas are generated, examined, reflected, developed, evaluated and ultimately realised. But they are not simply psychological faculties which are invoked when required, they are triggered and afforded by external props or stories (such as those design props (above) afford).

Indeed, a number of researchers have begun to conceptualise this "design imagination" as something which takes the form of reflexive conversations whether between people or between persons and their artefacts (Bucciarelli 1988; Schön 1983). With this comes the notions of perspective shifting and seeing (the design) as.

In this context, it has been argued that design communication is better thought of as "productive force" (Dong 2007, p. 5) that constitutes rather than merely expresses the design object. This view is consistent with the notion that thought is disclosed in the materiality of communication rather than preceding it (Merleau-Ponty 1945; Vygotsky 1987).

References

Akah B, Bardzell S (2010) Empowering products: personal identity through the act of appropriation. In: Proceedings of CHI 2010, pp 4021–4026

Akama Y, Ivanka T (2010) What community? facilitating awareness of 'community' through playful triggers. In: Proceedings of the 11th biennial participatory design conference, Nov 2010. ACM, pp 11–20

Ameel L, Tani S (2011) Everyday aesthetics in action: parkour eyes and the beauty of concrete walls. Emot Space Soc 9(3):1–10

Arvola M, Artman H (2007) Enactments in interaction design: how designers make sketches behave. Artifact: J Des Pract 1(2):106–119

Bal M (1997) Narratology: introduction to the theory of narrative, 2nd edn. University of Toronto Press, Toronto

Bannon L, Bødker S (1991) Beyond the interface: encountering artifacts in use. In: Carroll JM (ed) Designing interaction: psychology at the human–computer interface. CUP, Cambridge, pp 227–253

Bardzell J, Bardzell S, Lin C, Lindtner S, Toombs A (2017) HCI's making agendas. Foundations and Trends®. Human-Computer Interaction 11(3):126–200

Belin A, Prié Y (2012) DIAM: towards a model for describing appropriation processes through the evolution of digital artifacts. In: Proceedings of DIS '12: proceedings of the designing interactive systems conference 2012, 11–15 June 2012. Newcastle, UK, pp 645–654

Benford S, Giannachi G, Koleva B, Rodden T (2009) From interaction to trajectories: designing coherent journeys through user experiences. In: Proceedings of the SIGCHI conference on human factors in computing systems, Apr 2009. ACM, pp 709–718

Blom J, Monk A (2003) A theory of personalisation: why people personalise their PCs and mobile phones. Hum Comput Interact 18:193–228

Blythe MA, Dearden A (2008) Representing older people: towards meaningful images of the user in design scenarios. Univers Access Inf Soc. http://dx.doi.org/10.1007/s10209-008-0128-x

Bødker S, Klokmose CN (2012) Dynamics in artifact ecologies. In: Proceedings of NordiCHI '12, pp 448–457

Bucciarelli LL (1988) An ethnographic perspective on engineering design. Des Stud 9(3):159–168

Burns C, Dishman E, Verplank W, Lassiter B (1994) Actors, hairdos & videotape—informance design. In Conference companion on Human factors in computing systems, pp 119–120

Byrne A (1993) Truth in fiction: the story continued. Australas J Philos 71(1):24–35

Carroll JM (ed) (1995) Scenario-based design: envisioning work and technology in system development. Wiley, New York

Carroll J (2004) Completing design in use: closing the appropriation cycle. In: Proceedings of European conference on information systems, pp 337–347

Childress H (2004) Teenagers, territory and the appropriation of space. Childhood 11(2):195–205

Clark A (1998) Being there: putting brain, body, and world together again. MIT press

Cohn M (2004) User stories applied: for agile software development. Addison-Wesley Professional

Cooper A (1999) The inmates are running the asylum. Macmillan

Currie G (1990) The nature of fiction. Cambridge University Press

Darke J (1979) The primary generator and the design process. Des stud 1(1):36–44

Debord G (1967) Society of the Spectacle. Black and Red, Detroit

DeSanctis G, Poole MS (1994) Capturing the complexity in advanced technology use: adaptive structuration theory. Organ Sci 5(2):121–147

Dix A (2007) Designing for appropriation. In Proceedings of the 21st British HCI Group Annual Conference on People and Computers: HCI vol 2, BCS Learning & Development Ltd pp 27–30

Donald M (1991) Origins of the modern mind: three stages in the evolution of culture and cognition. Harvard University Press

Donald M (1993) Human cognitive evolution: what we were, what we are becoming. Soc Res 143–170

Dong A (2007) The enactment of design through language. Des Stud 28(1):5–21

Dourish P (2003) The appropriation of interactive technologies: some lessons from placeless documents. Comput Support Coop Work 12(4):465–490

Dreyfuss H (1955) Designing for people. Erni Peter, New York

Durrant AC, Kirk DS, Moncur W, Orzech KM, Taylor R, Pisanty DT (2018) Rich pictures for stakeholder dialogue: a polyphonic picture book. Des Stud 56:122–148

Fallman D (2003) Design-oriented human-computer interaction. In Proceedings of the SIGCHI conference on human factors in computing systems pp 225–232

Falzone A, Ahrens J, Nazer D, Rutledge V, Alinder Z, Polito J, McCutchen B (2011) The Andy Warhol Foundation for the Visual Arts brief of amicus curiae in support of defendants-appelants and urging reversal Patrick Cariou v Richard Prince and Gargosian Gallery Inc. http://www.scribd.com/doc/71837645/Cariou-v-Prince-Warhol-Foundation-Amicus-Brief. Accessed 8 Oct 2014

Garau M, Widenfeld HR, Antley A, Friedman D, Brogni A, Slater M (2004) Temporal and spatial variations in presence: a qualitative analysis. In Proceedings of the seventh international workshop on presence, pp 232–239

Garvey C (1990) Play. Harvard University Press, Cambridge

Gatzia DE, Sotnak E (2014) Fictional truth and make-believe. Philosophia 42(2):349–361

Gaver B, Dunne T, Pacenti E (1999) Design: cultural probes. interactions 6(1):21–29

Gaver W, Boucher A, Pennington S, Walker B (2004) Cultural probes and the value of uncertainty. Interact-Funology 11(5):53–56

Gibson JJ (1977) The theory of affordances. In: Shaw RE, Bransford J (eds) Perceiving, acting, and knowing. Lawrence Erlbaum Associates, Hillsdale, NJ

Giddens A (1984) The constitution of society: outline of the theory of structuration. University of California Press

Goodman J (2011) Pretense theory and the imported background. Open J Philos 1(1):22–25

Goldschmidt G (1991) The dialectics of sketching. Des Stud 4(2):123–143

Goldschmidt G (2003) The backtalk of self-generated sketches. Des Issues 19(1):72–88

Goldstein TR, Bloom P (2011) The mind on stage: why cognitive scientists should study acting. Trends Cogn Sci 15(4):141–142

Granic I, Lobel A, Engels RC (2014) The benefits of playing video games. Am Psychol 69(1):66

Graw I (2004) Dedication replacing appropriation: fascination, subversion and dispossession in appropriation art. In: Lawler L, Kaiser P (eds) Louise Lawler and others. Ostfildern-Ruit, Basel

Haesen M, Meskens J, Luyten K, Coninx K (2010) Draw me a storyboard: incorporating principles & techniques of comics. In: Proceedings of the 24th BCS interaction specialist group conference. British Computer Society, pp 133–142

Halskov K, Dalsgård P (2006) Inspiration card workshops. In: Proceedings of the 6th conference on designing interactive systems, June 2006. ACM, pp 2–11

Harris, P. L. (1998). Fictional absorption: Emotional responses to make-believe. Intersubjective communication and emotion in early ontogeny, 336-353.

Hart J (1998) The art of the storyboard: storyboarding for film, tv, and animation. Focal Press

Howard S, Carroll J, Murphy J, Peck J (2002). Using 'endowed props' in scenario-based design. In: Proceedings of the second Nordic conference on human-computer interaction, Oct 2002. ACM, pp 1–10

Hughes FP (1999) Children, play, and development. Allyn and Bacon, Needham Heights

Jent JF, Niec LN, Baker SE (2011) Play and interpersonal processes. Play in clinical practice: evidence-based approaches. Guilford Press, New York

Johansson M, Arvola M (2007a) A case study of how user interface sketches, scenarios and computer prototypes structure stakeholder meetings. In: Ball LJ, Sasse MA, Sas TC

Johansson M, Arvola M (2007b) A case study of how user interface sketches, scenarios and computer prototypes structure stakeholder meetings. In: Proceedings of the 21st British HCI group annual conference on people and computers: HCI... but not as we know it-vol 1, Sept 2007. British Computer Society, pp 177–184

Jones PH (2013) Design for care, 155-60. Rosenfeld Media, Brooklyn, NY

Karat C-M, Karat J (1992) Some dialogue on scenarios. ACM SIGCHI Bull 24(4):7

Kirsh D (1996) Adapting the environment instead of oneself. Adapt Behav 4(3/4):415–452

Kirsh D (2010) Thinking with external representations. AI Soc 25(4):441–454

Lawson (2006) How designers think

Leslie AM (1987) Pretense and representation: the origins of "theory of mind". Psych Rev 94:412–426

Lewis DK (1983) Truth in Fiction. reprinted with postscripts in philosophical papers vol.1, Oxford University Press

Loi D (2007) Reflective probes, primitive probes and playful triggers. In Ethnographic praxis in industry conference proceedings, vol 1, pp 232–245. Oxford, UK: Blackwell Publishing Ltd

Lucero A, Arrasvuori J (2010) PLEX cards: a source of inspiration when designing for playfulness. In: Proceedings of the 3rd international conference on fun and games. ACM, pp 28–37

MacLean A, Carter K, Lövstrand L, Moran T (1990) User-tailorable systems: pressing the issues with buttons, pp 175–182

Merleau-Ponty M (1945) Phénoménologie de la perception, Paris

Mithen SJ (2001) The evolution of imagination: an archaeological perspective. SubStance 30(1):28–54

Nelson HG, Stolterman E (2003a) Design judgement: decision-making in the 'real' world. Des J 6(1):23–31

Nelson HG, Stolterman E (2003b) The design way: intentional change in an unpredictable world: foundations and fundamentals of design competence. Educational Technology

Nielsen L (2014) Personas. The encyclopaedia of human-computer interaction, 2nd edn. Interaction design foundation. www.interaction-design.org/literature/book/the-encyclopedia-of-human-computer-interaction-2nd-ed/personas. Accessed Oct 2019

Orlikowski WJ (1992) The duality of technology: rethinking the concept of technology in organizations. Organ Sci 3(3), 398–427

Oulasvirta A, Kurvinen E, Kankainen T (2003) Understanding contexts by being there: case studies in bodystorming. Pers Ubiquit Comput 7(2):125–134

Porfirio D, Fisher E, Sauppé A, Albarghouthi A, Mutlu B (2019) Bodystorming human-robot interactions. In: Proceedings of the 32nd annual ACM symposium on user interface software and technology. ACM, pp 479–491

Russ SW (2004) Play in child development and psychotherapy. Erlbaum, Mahwah

Rutherford MD, Young GS, Hepburn S, Rogers SJ (2007) A longitudinal study of pretend play in autism. J Autism Dev Disord 37(6):1024–1039

Ryan ML (2008) Interactive narrative, plot types, and interpersonal relations. Springer, Berlin, Heidelberg, pp 6–13

Salovaara A (2008) Inventing new uses for tools: a cognitive foundation for studies on appropriation. Hum Technol 4(2):209–228

Salovaara A, Höök K, Cheverst K, Twidale M, Chalmers M, Sas C (2011) Appropriation and creative use: linking user studies and design. In: CHI 2011 workshop. CHI 2011, 7–12 May 2011, Vancouver, BC, Canada. ACM 978-1-4503-0268-5/11/05

Scaife M, Rogers Y (1996) External cognition: how do graphical representations work? Int J Hum-Comput Stud 45(2):185–213

Schaeffer J-M (2013) Fictional vs. Factual Narration. In: Hühn, Peter et al. (eds) The living handbook of narratology. Hamburg: Hamburg University. http://www.lhn.uni-hamburg.de/article/fictional-vs-factual-narration

Schneider A (2003) On 'appropriation'. A critical reappraisal of the concept and its application in global art practices. Soc Anthropol 11(2):215–229

Searle JR (1979) What is an intentional state? Mind 88(349):74–92

Seja AL, Russ SW (1999) Children's fantasy play and emotional understanding. J Clin Child Psychol 28(2):269–277

Sengers P, Gaver B (2006) Staying open to interpretation: engaging multiple meanings in design and evaluation. In: Carroll JM, Bødker S, Coughlin J (eds) Proceedings of DIS'06, pp 99–108

Silverstone R, Haddon L (1996) Design and the domestication of information and communication technologies: technical change and everyday life. In: Mansell R, Silverstone R (eds) Communication by design. OUP, NY, pp 44–74

Singer JL, Singer DG (2005) Preschoolers' imaginative play as precursor of narrative consciousness. Imagin, Cogn Pers 25(2):97–117

Sirkin, D., & Ju, W. (2014, October). Using embodied design improvisation as a design research tool. In Proceedings of the international conference on Human Behavior in Design (HBiD 2014). Ascona, Switzerland

Sleeswijk Visser F, Van der Lugt R, Stappers PJ (2004) The personal cardset—a designer-centred tool for sharing insights from user studies. In: Proceedings of second international conference on appliance design, pp 157–158

Spinosa C, Flores F, Dreyfus HL (1997) Disclosing new worlds: entrepreneurship, democratic action, and the cultivation of solidarity. MIT Press, Cambridge, MA

Sterling B (2005) Shaping things. MIT Press, Cambridge

Stout WF (2003) IDEO method cards: 51 ways to inspire design. IDEO

Suwa M, Gero, JS, Purcell T (1998) The roles of sketches in early conceptual design processes. In: Proceedings of twentieth annual meeting of the cognitive science society. Lawrence Erlbaum Hillsdale, New Jersey, pp 1043–1048

Svanæs D, Seland G (2004) Putting the users center stage: role playing and low-fi prototyping enable end users to design mobile systems, pp 479–486

Technology Strategy Board (2010). https://www.gov.uk/government/publications/technology-strategy-board-annual-report-and-accounts-2010-to-2011

Toon A (2010) Models as make-believe. In: Beyond mimesis and convention. Springer, Netherlands, pp 71–96

Truong KN, Hayes GR, Abowd GD (2006) Storyboarding: an empirical determination of best practices and effective guidelines. In: Proceedings of the 6th conference on designing interactive systems, June 2006. ACM, pp 12–21

Turner P, Harviainen JT (2016) Digital Make-Believe. Springer International Publishing

Van der Lelie C (2006) The value of storyboards in the product design process. Pers Ubiquit Comput 10(2–3):159–162

Velt R, Benford S, Reeves S (2017). A survey of the trajectories conceptual framework: investigating theory use in HCI. In: Proceedings of the 2017 CHI conference on human factors in computing systems, May 2017. ACM, pp 2091–2105

Vincent CJ, Blandford A (2015) Usability standards meet scenario-based design: challenges and opportunities. J Biomed Inform 53:243–250

von Slatt J (2007) Steampunk desktop, image available at https://www.flickr.com/photos/16307058@N00/2848341848/in/photolist

Vygotsky L (1987) Zone of proximal development. Mind in society: the development of higher psychological processes 5291:157

Walton KL (1990) Mimesis as make-believe: on the foundations of the representational arts. Harvard University Press, Cambridge, MA

Warhol A (1962) Campbell's Soup Cans MoMA., New York

Wölfel C, Merritt T (2013) Method card design dimensions: a survey of card-based design tools. In: IFIP conference on human-computer interaction, Sept 2013. Springer, Berlin, Heidelberg, pp 479–486

Yilmaz S, Daly SR, Seifert CM, Gonzalez R (2016) Evidence-based design heuristics for idea generation. Des Stud 46:95–124

Young RM, Barnard P (1987) The use of scenarios in human-computer interaction research: turbocharging the tortoise of cumulative science. In: Proceedings of the SIGCHI/GI conference 1987, pp 291–296

Yuill S (2001) JODI: untitled-game, presented at Words and Things, CCA: Glasgow, 17th November 2001. available from http://www.lipparosa.org/essays/jodi_talk.pdf

Zang N, Rosson MB, Nasser V (2008) Mashups: who? what? why? In: Proceedings of conference on human factors in computing systems, extended abstracts on human factors in computing systems. Florence, Italy, pp 3171–3176

Chapter 4
Aesthetics and Imagination

Chapter Thumbnail

While recent years have witnessed an "aesthetic turn" in HCI, we are still awaiting the arrival of an agreed "digital aesthetics". However, it is widely recognised that aesthetics have an important role in the overall experience of digital technology and that they may also be the single most important factor in deciding which (say) mobile phone to buy. While this may seem a very specific example, phones have proved to be the most ubiquitous of all digital artefacts, and we buy on them on basis of how they look.

Yet despite the importance of aesthetics, no one (inevitably) can agree quite what they are, why we seem to be geared towards them (why, for example, 17,000 years ago were the good people of Lascaux painting the walls of caves rather than inventing the wheel?). Aesthetics have attracted a great number of musings, "slogans" and even factor analytic treatments, for example, the German philosopher Immanuel Kant wrote that the imagination provides for 'free play' with aesthetics to create an affective state with a positive valence (that is, and I paraphrase, attractive things make us feel good); Norman has proposed that "attractive things are easy to use" while Hassenzahl has argued that the aesthetics enable us to identify with them and/or be stimulated by them ("we find attractive things, attractive"). We are very good (that is, both quick and accurate) at judging the attractiveness of people (their faces in particular) and this ability may be in play when we make judgements about digital technology. And of course, our interest here is again confined to the interplay between imagination and aesthetics.

Our approach in this chapter is to treat imagination as *seeing-as*, that is, by adopting an *aesthetic* perspective rather than our usual veridical view of the world, we see artefacts, people, and events as attractive (or not) and consequently, a source of pleasure, easy to use or attractive. This is not and cannot be anything like a complete description of aesthetics but it does allow us to introduce imagination to the discussion in a coherent fashion. This is aesthetics, for example, as a source of appropriation; and aesthetics as a prop; and so forth.

© Springer Nature Switzerland AG 2020
P. Turner, *Imagination + Technology*, Human–Computer Interaction Series,
https://doi.org/10.1007/978-3-030-37348-1_4

4.1 Introduction

> The ascription of human-like characteristics to computing technology has become integral
> to our design, use, training, and communications with regard to computing technology and
> it has been argued to be the most common metaphor used in computing discourse.
>
> Johnson et al. (2008, p. 169)

Aesthetics has traditionally been concerned with the principles by which we appreciate and understand the nature of beauty and perhaps because of this, until quite recently, aesthetics has had only a peripheral role in HCI. As Hassenzahl (2004) notes, HCI has been, at best, a little uneasy with beauty, "If it is pretty, it won't work" and quotes Russo and De Moraes (2003, p. 146) who have observed that sometimes a pretty product is still accused of hiding "harm behind its beauty". Further, aesthetics has often been narrowly confined to how a user interface might look but this has changed.

Note: although this chapter discusses aesthetics from the perspective of imagination, there is quite a lot of background work on the former before we can get to the latter. Although a technology's aesthetics is all too often treated as though it were simply a matter of how something looks, as we will see, it is so very much more than this.

Nothing special

One question which is rarely asked is, "Can we reasonably apply the term aesthetics to digital artefacts?" Statistics reveal that Google was the most visited website in 2019,[1] but can its user interface design be described as aesthetically pleasing? Are its aesthetics relevant? Stolnitz (1969, p. 27) tells us that, "anything at all, whether sensed or perceived, whether it is the product of imagination or conceptual thought, can become the object of aesthetic attention". This observation also places both imagination and everyday technology such as smartphones, and websites squarely in the centre of this narrative. We might conclude that an aesthetic object is in no sense special. And aesthetics, of late, have attracted the attention of researchers who have written of it from widely divergent perspectives—for example, experimental, cognitive, marketing and evolutionary psychology have all contributed something from original empirical research through to extended thought experiments and detailed argumentation, as have researchers from product design, and the neurosciences (neuroaesthetics). The resulting definitions of aesthetics for HCI and digital product design are correspondingly complex and tend to favour the home discipline of the originator, for example, the psychologist and HCI researcher Hassenzahl (2008, p. 291) defines aesthetics as the "predominantly affect-driven evaluative response to the visual Gestalt of an object", which is a predominately psychological-driven definition. The HCI specialist Donald Norman, by contrast, describes aesthetics in terms being easier to use "attractive things work better" (Norman 2004).

---

[1] http://www.ebizmba.com/articles/most-popular-websites.

What of imagination? Well, unlike many other areas of HCI, imagination and make-believe have already been acknowledged to have roles. Walton, for example, has argued at length that we appreciate aesthetics by way of make-believe and imagination is frequently mentioned alongside the rhetoric surrounding perceived, anticipated or the expected (collectively, the imagined) use of a digital artefact.

Historically, the psychological study of aesthetics began with Fechner in the 1870s who developed the conceptual foundations for understanding both art and aesthetics. However, this was not to flourish due to the heavy hands of the Behaviourists (say between 1910 and 1950). The psychologist Berlyne (1974) was to revive the empirical interest in art by creating his own theoretical framework based around an arousal-pleasure dimension which, in some regards, parallels Hassenzahl's (2004) contemporary work on hedonism.

More recently, psychologists Leder and Nadal (2014) have usefully distinguished between art and aesthetics. Art, they tell us, is often appreciated for reasons other than its aesthetics and write that the psychology of art, "aims to characterise the psychological mechanisms involved in the appreciation of art, such as grasping an artwork's symbolism, identifying its compositional resources, or relating to it to its historical context" (p. 445). In contrast, the psychology of aesthetics, "aims to identify and describe the psychological mechanisms that allow humans to experience and appreciate a broad variety of objects and phenomena, including utensils (sic), commodities, designs, other people, or nature, in aesthetic terms (beautiful, attractive, ugly, sublime, picturesque and so on)".

4.2 Seeing it as Something Special

People, as Santayana has observed, are drawn to the aesthetic features of objects and the environment around them, writing, "*In all products of human industry we notice the keenness with which the eye is attracted to the mere appearance of things: great sacrifices of time and labour are made to it in the most vulgar manufactures … There must therefore be in our nature a very radical and wide-spread tendency to observe beauty, and to value it. No account of the principles of the mind can be at all adequate that passes over so conspicuous a faculty*" (Santayana 1896/1955). Dutton (2009) called it the *art instinct*.

Aesthetics speak directly to us and influence our affective responses ("they make us happy"), and behaviour ("we find them easier to use"), and as we have already noted, shape our choice of products ("they make us buy them") e.g., Reimann et al. (2010), Van der Laan et al. (2012). And, this is quite understandable from the perspective of design at least, because, "Good design at the front-end suggests that everything is in order at the back-end, whether or not that is the case" and conversely, "Problems with visual design can turn users off so quickly that they never discover all the smart choices you made with navigation or interaction design." (Design Council 2017). The public would seem to be in step with these observations as 77% of people agree with the statement, "people work more productively in well-designed offices" and

72% of people agree that "well-designed houses will increase in value quicker than average". And Bloch (1995) observes that "a good design attracts consumers to a product, communicates to them, and adds value to the product by increasing the quality of the usage experiences associated with it" (p. 16), citing examples ranging from Swatch® wristwatches, to the early Apple Macintosh® computers, and the continued appeal of the venerable Rolling Stones.

Designing and marketing aesthetic products is of growing importance in markets where many basic needs of consumers have been satisfied. As core product attributes, such as quality and functionality, become increasingly homogeneous (e.g. Reimann et al. 2010), vendors are differentiating themselves by focussing on less tangible features such as aesthetics (Brunner et al. 2009). For example, Coca-Cola have created "special limited-edition" designs of their famous curved bottle for special events ("the Olympics") or times of the year ("the holidays"). Aesthetics have become a reliable differentiating attribute (e.g. Zolli 2004). This trend towards aesthetics in product differentiation may be based on the insight that regardless of the consumption domain, aesthetic designs seem to trigger certain positive responses in consumers such as an immediate desire to own the product (Norman 2004); a higher willingness to pay for it (Bloch et al. 2003); and an increased inclination to show off and care for that product (Bloch 1995). More importantly, while products purchased solely for their functional utility may lose their appeal when becoming technically obsolete, products with aesthetic qualities may be treasured long after their functional value fades (Martin 1998).

The psychology of aesthetic experience

We begin with Beardsley's (1969) definition of aesthetic experience which is, "A person is having an aesthetic experience during a particular stretch of time if and only if the greater part of his mental activity during that time is united and made pleasurable by being tied to the form and qualities of a sensuously presented or imaginatively intended object on which his primary attention is concentrated".

Levinson's (1996) more recent conception of aesthetic pleasure also relies on psychological processes: "Pleasure in an object is aesthetic when it derives from apprehension and reflection on the object's individual character and content, both for itself and in relation to the structural base on which it rests" (Levinson 1996).

Cinzia and Vittorio (2009, p. 682) define an aesthetic experience as to "perceive-feel-sense" which foregrounds the respective roles of the sensorimotor, emotional and cognitive systems. Chatterjee (2011) prefers to define it as "the perception, production, and response to art, as well as interactions with object and scenes that evoke an intense feeling, often of pleasure". In contrast, Bergeron and Lopes (2012) suggest that there are three dimensions to an aesthetic experience, namely, the evaluative, the phenomenological (or affective) and a semantic dimension. They also note that there is no reason to suppose that all three dimensions are required in every instance. Chatterjee and Vartanian (2014) also offer their own "aesthetic triad" proposal (this time from a neurological perspective) suggesting that aesthetic experiences arise from the interaction among sensory-motor, emotion-valuation and meaning-knowledge neural systems.

These six definitions are all thoughtful, theoretically grounded and have empirical support and they are all different. And there seems no good reason to prefer one over another. However, perhaps the most comprehensive treatment of aesthetic experiences is from Leder et al. (2004) which was reviewed and revised in 2014 (Leder and Nadal 2014) in the light of new experimental methods which were developed in the interim. An aesthetic experience, Leder tell us, begins before the actual perception, with the "social discourse that configures expectations, anticipations, and an aesthetic orientation" (p. 445). another way of phrasing this is to recognise that people will have had imagined how it will be. An aesthetic experience also occurs in context, which also serves to shape those expectations and orientation, and to create an environment that can contribute to heightening the artistic status of an object.

Unlike many other accounts, Leder's model situates the psychological mechanisms in context—the others, like so many psychological theories are divorced from the untidiness of the real world. The model is complex and if we confine ourselves to the psychological aspects, we can see that in relies on several stages of perceptual processing which is concerned with grouping, symmetry analysis, and a range of other perceptual features that are relevant to aesthetic appreciation. The next stage involves the analysis of familiarity, prototypicality and meaning and the integration of information from memory. Finally, the "output" from the cognitive system is an aesthetic judgement while the affective system produces an "aesthetic emotion", although how this might be different from a simple, everyday emotion is not described.

The savanna hypothesis

From another perspective, our aesthetic sense is a product of our evolution and to understand it, as Dutton puts it, we need to "reverse-engineer" it to explain how it evolved. So, we will approach the origins of aesthetics from an evolutionary psychological perspective. The use of this kind of analysis prompts a caveat. While it must be the case that any given specific sense or capability is the product of our evolution, it is difficult to avoid the feeling that we are reading a modern "just-so" story, of the "the beginning of the armadillo". The usual starting point for this kind of analysis is to assume that the aesthetics sense provides a reproductive advantage to our ancestors, an example of which is that we find symmetry attractive in potential mates. This preference is supported by the evidence that facial symmetry, for example, is correlated with reproductive health (e.g. Scheib et al. 1999), and so it is plausible that preferring symmetrical faces is an aesthetic adaptation that is likely to result in higher reproductive success (Thornhill and Gangestad 1993). Then, in the minds of evolutionary psychologists at least, this preference for symmetry can be seen as an adaptation which we have extend to the creation and enjoyment of works of art, entertainment and the design of the latest smart phone. (We return to this discussion in Sect. 4.6).

However, Dutton (2009) reminds us that evolution has at its disposal a number of different mechanisms, namely, natural selection and sexual selection. Natural selection relies on random mutation and selective retention and can explain our fondness for fast food and sugary snacks and our revulsion at the smell of rotting meat, or our fear of spiders. However, sexual selection contradicts this, and the most famous example is the origins of the peacock's exuberant tail. The tail did not evolve for survival (as it is cumbersome and awkward) but instead it is the result of the mating choices made by peahens. Peahens prefer flashy tails (the more eye spots the better), so peacocks with such tails have a chance to reproduce with spot-loving peahens before being eaten by the local wild dogs. Thus, the experience of beauty is one of the ways that evolution has of arousing and sustaining interest, in order to encourage us toward making the most adaptive decisions for survival and reproduction or has he puts it, "Beauty is nature's way of acting at a distance".

4.3   The Aesthetic Turn in HCI

HCI has a fondness for turning. It has successively turned, that is, focussed its research/design attention on the contextual; the social; the corporeal; the experiential; the "green" and, of course, it has quite recently turned its attention to the aesthetic. These turns are typically associated with special issues of journals and the appearance of scholarly publications with titles like "a research agenda for ..." whatever the Zeitgeist happens to be, and before, or just after, the appearance of the next turn. After a year or two when sufficient work has been reported, someone will write a retrospective reflecting and making sense of the previous excitement. A good example of this is Udsen and Jørgensen (2005), reflecting on what they describe as the "blurred picture" which aesthetics presents. They have duly claimed that we have witnessed a turn to the aesthetic within HCI, and have argued that this has taken four forms, which they identified as "cultural", "functionalist" "experiential" and what they describe the "techno-futurist". While this is by no means the last word on the subject and will undoubtedly be subject to revision, it does serve to present a picture of where and how interest in aesthetics in HCI has fallen. These four different forms appear to be analogous with the different schools in art—for example, the impressionists as versus the cubist and so forth.

"Cultural aesthetics"
Udsen and Jørgensen highlight Brenda Laurel whose most celebrated work which was to show a parallel between the use of technology and a theatrical performance (Computers as Theatre, 1993). She has also suggested that interactive systems should provide the users with "pleasurable engagement" through the use of interface metaphors of "both emotional and intellectual appeal". In all, she argued for the user interface to be treated as an "expressive form" and a hybrid of cultural experimentation and emerging (HCI) standards. This form of aesthetics is derived from the humanities and "new media" and provides a non-informational space rather than a neutral screen representation (e.g. icons representing files, trees showing directory structures and some such). As is apparent this aesthetic may be better suited to installations rather than desktops or on mobile devices—the aesthetics of "digital art" rather than workaday report writing.

"Functionalist aesthetics"

Alongside this is the functionalist approach typified by Jordan's *Designing Pleasurable Products* (2003) which explores the relationship between product design and user pleasure and the ACM Designing Pleasurable Products and Interfaces (DPPI) series of conferences (2003–2013). DPPI described itself as a leading venue for designers, artists, psychologists, systems engineers, social scientists and many more to come together to debate and define future design research and practice. In many ways this is aesthetics for enhanced usability, most neatly captured in Norman's "attractive things work better".

"Experientialist aesthetics"

The experiential approach is not so much concerned with issues such as usability and utility and engaging with "promoting new ways of communicating immaterial messages and experiences through emotional frictions, engaging interactions and seductive means" (p. 209). Add to this the recurrent theme of aesthetic interaction "fostering technologies that inform, challenge, delight and excite" and we have an outline of the experiential approach to aesthetics! We do, of course, include persuasive technology which serve to prompt, shape and direct user responses. They offer a "classic" example of this, in Plumbdesign's Visual Thesaurus which shows the result of a text search as a "moving, organic structure that encourages users to examine related words"—the visual presentation acting as the vehicle of seduction (Khaslavsky and Shedroff 1999).

"Techno-futurist aesthetics"

The final category is described as "techno-futurist" which is described as being "philosophically inspired". The authors cast their net widely to include the philosophical thoughts of Paul Dourish; the visionary description of what is now Ubi-Com when technology becomes truly ubiquitous (Weiser 1999), and Ishii's work on Tangible Bits (the use of really physical user interfaces); and whatever is yet to come.

While recognising that these four forms have their own philosophies, traditions and have been realised in different kinds of user interfaces, Udsen and Jørgensen also conclude that the aesthetics of these digital products is now just a matter of everyday life which is very much the perspective we have adopted reflecting the work of Hallnäs and Redström, and Petersen. So, what does this all mean to the user of technology? The authors conclude that users will not be valued more, nor will we have new evaluative frameworks, instead we have recognised that this is a broader and more meaningful meeting of human and machine. With this, we may have to wait for the next review.

Emotional design

Norman has told us unequivocally that attractive things work better (2004), implying, perhaps, that aesthetics (by way of affectivity) trumps usability. This claim has important consequences and may have had its origins with the work of two Japanese researchers, Kuroso and Kashimura (1995) and the subsequent work of Tractinsky in Israel. The Japanese researchers developed and evaluated a number of different ATM (cash machines) keypad layouts which were identical in function, the number of buttons how they worked, but differed in the attractiveness of the layout. They found that the attractively presented layouts were easier to use than the functionally equivalent unattractive ATMs. The story, as Norman tells it that these results intrigued the Israeli researcher Noam Tractinsky who assumed that the experiment was flawed. Perhaps, he is said to have thought, the result would be true of Japanese, but this could not be true of Israelis. He suggested that as aesthetic preferences are culturally dependent and "Japanese culture is known for its aesthetic tradition," but Israelis? Israelis, he tells us, are action oriented—they don't care about beauty (his words). So Tractinsky replicated the experiment after obtaining the Japanese ATM layouts, translating the Japanese into Hebrew, and designed a new experiment, with rigorous methodological controls. However, not only did he replicate the Japanese findings, but the results were stronger in Israel than in Japan, contrary to his belief that beauty and function "… were not expected to correlate".

Norman's subsequent work has been to investigate the role of aesthetics in design from the perspective of our affective response to it. He reasons that it is our emotional systems which provide us with feedback when we are solving problems—such as making sense of a digital product. So, he argues, if we like the appearance of a digital product, this produces a change to our emotional state which is communicated to our cognitive system. Norman elaborates, telling us that, "what many people don't realize is that there is a strong emotional component to how products are designed and put to use" (p. 5), and that "the emotional design side of design may be more critical to a product's success than its practical elements". So, this is why he tells us that attractive things work better and why his book on aesthetics is entitled *Emotional Design*.

A three-layer model

His emotional design comprises the visceral, the behavioural and the reflective levels. We should, of course, recognise that Norman is writing about design and not about psychology, but it is worth noting that his model appears to correspond closely to the triune model of the brain as proposed by MacLean (1990). The triune brain account sees it as consisting of three phylogenetically distinct complexes or groups of neural structures. The most ancient is the reptilian complex (the R-complex), next is the paleo-mammalian complex (limbic system), and finally the youngest is the neo-mammalian complex (neocortex). It is proposed that these structures have evolved sequentially. Although this is no longer held to be an accurate account of the development of the brain, it has proved to be popular and enduring in popular science.

Anyway, back to Norman's model. What he describes as the visceral level corresponds to the first impressions of a product. At this level people do not think about a product, but spontaneously judge, if they like or dislike it. The visceral level is independent of cultural aspects and is equal for everyone. Norman describes it as "genetically determined" (p. 29). This definition distinguishes the operation of the visceral level from other treatments of first impressions. The visceral level does not reason (because it cannot) and, instead, works by "pattern matching". Norman then provides (which he describes as his "best guesses") two lists of situations and objects which we are genetically programmed to like or dislike: we like "warm, comfortably lit places, caresses, attractive people and rounded, smooth objects". We dislike "sudden, unexpected loud sounds or bright lights, looming objects (that is, things which appear to be about to hit the observer), sharp objects, misshaped human bodies and snakes and spiders". Norman concludes that these are pre-dispositions rather than fully fledged mechanisms.

This next level of design is about use and is described as the behavioural level. He writes that people may seek to appraise a product's functionality and issues such as ease of use of the product come to the fore. This level of use corresponds to what Norman describes in detail in *The Psychology of Everyday Design* (1988). While Norman calls this the behavioural level it might also be called the cognitive except that he introduces an incongruous aesthetic element. He suggests that function, understandability and usability are three of the four major components of this level—which is consistent with his treatment of mental models and then adds "physical feel" as a four component. He also specifically uses the image of someone showering and enjoying "the sensual pleasure, the feel—quite literally—of the water streaming across the body" (p. 70). Yet on the page before, he tells us that on this level, "Appearances does not really matter" (p. 69). So, visual appeal—classical aesthetics do not seem to be relevant here but haptic appeal—embodied aesthetics (perhaps)—are. This is a little difficult to square with his assertion that "Attractive things work better" which explicitly links appearance and use.

Finally, comes the reflective level which "covers a lot of territory. It is all about message, about culture, and about the meaning of a product or its use. For one, it is about the meaning of things, the personal remembrances something evokes. For another, very different things, it is about self-image and the message a product sends to others". So, at this level, consciousness takes part in the process, with people actively endeavouring to understand and interpret things often in the context of past experiences and imagined future actions.

Aesthetics as a defining aspect of user experience

Hallnäs and Redström (2002) write that they recognise that with the growing ubiquity of computational things, that we need to focus on what it means for something to be present in our lives, as opposed to something we just use.

They suggest the terms "use" and "presence" to distinguish between the two and we should note that this is yet another reminder that interaction is an inadequate description of our relationship with digital products. While use refers to a general description of a thing in terms of how it is employed, presence refers to existential definitions of a thing based on how we invite and accept it as a part of our digital world. From this perspective, they see aesthetics as providing a rationale for the choices we make. Interestingly, their description of use and presence appears to be the reverse of Heidegger's famous ready-to-hand and present-at-hand.

Petersen et al. (2004) also distinguish between what they describe as "aesthetic interaction" and pragmatist aesthetics (cf. Shusterman 1992). They write, "In a pragmatist perspective aesthetics is a part of everyday life. It stems from a use-relationship. Aesthetic interaction comprises the views that aesthetics is instrumental and that artefacts are appropriated in use." Continuing this theme, Petersen et al. (2008) have also observed that the ubiquity of digital technology in everyday life has changed the ways in which we interact with it. As computer systems change from being very specific tools for work to ubiquitous computational objects, the nature of the interaction changes too. They quote the work of Redström (2008) who has observed that "We are dealing with new devices and new qualities of use which are [...] related to emotional qualities, to experiential qualities, and to aesthetic qualities ...".

In contrast, to treat aesthetics as a pattern of use or perception or appearance, Lavie and Tractinsky (2004) have sought to differentiate between classical and expressive aesthetics. The former, they describe as referring to traditional aesthetic notions which emphasises orderly and clear design, while expressive aesthetics is associated with the design's creativity and originality. Classical aesthetics embraces principles such as consistency and the use of a structured layout, symmetry, clean and clear design (this is quite like the definition of use proposed by Hallnäs and Redström); whereas expressive aesthetics is "manifested by the designer's creativity and originality and by the ability to interface qualities, such as "beautiful", "challenging" and "fascinating" (again, recalling "presence").

Finally, Ulrich (2006) defines the aesthetics of an artefact as the immediate feelings evoked when experiencing it via the sensory system. He considers aesthetic responses to be different from (other) cognitive responses in that they are rapid and involuntary. Indeed, this is a description of our first impressions which are very rapid and non-cognitive. Aesthetic responses are an aggregate assessment biased either positively (e.g., beauty or attraction) or negatively (e.g., ugliness or repulsion) and not a nuanced multi-dimensional evaluation.

Aesthetics and me

We find things aesthetically appealing if they allow us to express something about us. We make these appraisals by make-believing their use or ownership and in this section, we consider examples of how this has been studied.

Hassenzahl writes that our experience of interactive technology can be divided into two broad forms: the pragmatic and the hedonic. The former is concerned with users' goals and hence the usual array of utility (that is, answering the question, does this technology allow me to complete tasks?) and usability (does it allow me to complete tasks easily?). This is treating technology simply as a means to our ends. In contrast, the hedonic attributes of technology are primarily related to the users' sense of self, which Hassenzahl further subdivides into self-stimulation and self-identification. The stimulation aspect of technology is a measure of how much fun it is, or how interesting it is to use (we might think this as "engagement"). Identification is a little more interesting as it is concerned with the "human need to express one's self through objects". This self-presentational function of products is, he tells us, entirely social; individuals want to be seen in specific ways by relevant others. Using and possessing a product is a means to a desired self-presentation, that is, communicating important personal values to relevant others. The reference to self immediately implies a significant role for imagination (as mental time travel) at least when we are attempted to evaluate an item of technology. As ever, the recognition of the importance of imagination in these experiences is not voiced.

In one typical and noteworthy study, Hassenzahl (2004) was to explore the relationships among technology judged to have pragmatic, hedonic–stimulation, hedonic–identification attributes and was judged to be beautiful (or not) too. Given Norman's "attractive things are easier to use" we might expect that beautiful products to be judged to be more usable than those to be judged unattractive.

The subject of the study was MP3-player software with different "skins". A skin is a graphics file used to change the appearance of an application's user interface. The Sonique skins used here varied in presentational style and perceived usability (due to, for example, differences in layout, legibility, positioning of controls and so forth), while the purpose and functionality remain constant.

Prior to the study proper there was a pre-test to establish the base-line attractiveness of the skins. To this end, the participants were invited to judge the "skins" to be beautiful or unattractive. This assessment was elicited using a questionnaire with a 7-point bipolar scale with the verbal anchors ugly and beautiful.

Based on these pre-test ratings, the two least attractive (specifically the skins labelled Danzig, w98) and the two most beautiful (ts2-Razor, QuickSkin) skins were selected. The AttracDiff 2 questionnaire[2] was then employed to investigate these further. The questionnaire was used to measure the skins' *perceived* pragmatic quality (PQ), their *perceived* hedonic quality–stimulation (HQS) and their *perceived* hedonic quality-identification (HQI). A series of analyses of variance were conducted on these data which revealed that the attributions of beautiful—unattractive were confirmed. However, while previous research had suggested a clear relation between usability and attractiveness, no such evidence was found here.

Instead goodness (satisfaction) was found to be a matter of perceived usability and was affected by actual use. In contrast, hedonic attributes and beauty remained stable over time.

Overall, the goodness and beauty of an artefact were judged to be different, he concluded that the nature of beauty is rather self-oriented than goal-oriented.

This finally, concludes our introductory sketch of aesthetics.

4.4 Make-Believe Aesthetics

Make-believe aesthetics has two distinct and unrelated forms. First there is Walton's make-believe account of representation to which we have made frequent reference in earlier chapters. Secondly, there is skeuomorphic design, which is better called skeuomorphic aesthetics and is regarded by many as being a matter of historical interest or one of legacy.

Walton (1993) writes, "Dolls and hobby horses are valuable for their contribution to make-believe. The same is true for paintings and novels. These and other

---

[2]The questionnaire consists of twenty-one 7-point items with bipolar verbal anchors.

props stimulate our imagination and provide for exciting or pleasurable or interesting engagements with fictional worlds. A doll, in itself just a bundle of rags or
moulded plastic, comes alive in a game of make-believe, providing the participant
with (fictional) baby". Walton calls this "prop-oriented make-believe". His interest
in "toys and art" arise from the earlier work of Gombrich (1963) on this very subject.
In his Meditations on a Hobby Horse Gombrich compares pictures of a horse to that
of a child's hobby horse. While a picture may accurately portray a horse, a hobby
horse, in contrast, is a substitute for a horse. He rejects the view that the hobby horse
is a symbol—standing for a horse—a man-made horse, as it were, he argues instead
that it can function as a horse. A hobby-horse can be ridden and more to the point
it can be ridden as part of a make-believe game and it is this last point that Walton
builds upon. In short, function trumps form, "Any ride-able object could serve as
a horse". Walton introduced the idea of fictional worlds to complete this picture.
The child's hobby horse is not just any old horse but can become Black Bess in the
fictional world in which the child is Dick Turpin on his way to rob a carriage. Walton
proposes that when we look at a picture, say of, Dali's Don Quixote we create a
fictional world in which we are looking at Don Quixote. But this is not the Spain of
Don Quixote as created by Dali, but a fictional world that includes Don Quixote and
the viewer.

Only a few decades ago, digital technology was unfamiliar and more than a little
intimidating for many people. If this technology was to deliver all that it promised, it
had to become familiar and easy to use and much of this challenge lay with the design
of the user interface—in short, how it looked and how it behaved. So, designers
hit upon the idea of making applications look like their real-world equivalent, or
something approximate. So was born skeuomorphic design. If an application looked
like (say) a book then the user might expect it to behave like a book and offer
affordances similar to a real book. User interface design thus acquired this gloss or
ornamentation. Continuing with the book theme, a notepad application might include
a cover, "paper" complete with lines and a watermark and perhaps with a "metal ring
binder" holding the pages together. It is assumed that as everyone has seen and used
a physical notebook, using the software equivalent should be easy.

So, in essence, skeuomorphs have been employed to make software applications look more familiar. Norman has described skeuomorphism in terms of cultural
constraints (by which he seems to mean conventions and has introduced the idea
of perceived affordance, where the user can tell what an object provides or does
based on its appearance alone. Though "perceived affordances" has been replaced
by "convention".

Skeuomorphic design involves make-believe aesthetics as it is concerned with
making something look like something else. So, everyday examples of this include
electric candles. An electric candle is an electric light which aesthetically has been
made to look as though it were a paraffin wax candle.

Skeuomorphs are all around us, enabling us to make-believe they are things that
they are not. And then they stopped being fashionable. Apple in the mid-2000s (or
so) dropped these often, over-elaborate representations for a simpler flat design. And
for the present, this approach to flat design continues. But skeuomorphs never really

disappeared. The shutter-click sound which accompanies taking a photograph with cellphones is one such example. The user interface for manipulating digital audio still employs make-believe control knobs and dials. A digital contact list still looks like a Rolodex (a design which dates from the 1950s). And we still step through a document on a phone or a tablet as though it were paper by swiping it.

4.5 Aesthetics and You

Theodor Lipps was a 19th century philosopher noted for his work on aesthetics. He delineated the concept of *Einfühlung* or empathy, defined as "projecting oneself onto the object of perception". Lipps closely linked our aesthetic perception and our perception of another embodied person as a minded creature. Thus, the nature of aesthetic empathy is always the "experience of another human". We appreciate another object as beautiful because empathy allows us to see it in analogy to another human body. Similarly, we recognize another organism as a minded creature because of empathy. Empathy in this context is more specifically understood as a phenomenon of "inner imitation," where my mind mirrors the mental activities or experiences of another person based on the observation of his bodily activities or facial expressions.

Empirical work has confirmed that a single glance of a face, enables people to appraise its attractiveness and make a range of social attributions (e.g. Olson and Marshuetz 2005; Bar et al. 2006; Willis and Todorov 2006; Todorov et al. 2009). For example, a 33-ms view of a face is sufficient for people to make a judgment as to their trustworthiness (Todorov et al. 2009). Additional time exposure only tends to confirm these first impressions (Willis and Todorov 2006). And these first impressions are formed very quickly, and enable us to determine accurately and reliably a surprising number of attributes of the person we are looking at. These include their sexual attractiveness (e.g. Berry 2000); and their sexual orientation (Rule and Ambady 2008); and physical attractiveness (Cunningham 1986), and their political affiliations (Ballew and Todorov 2007), a number of their personality traits (Borkenau et al. 2009), and their competence (Cuddy et al. 2008).

As Mende-Siedlecki et al. (2013) note, it was Asch (1948) who observed that, 'We look at a person and immediately a certain impression of his character forms itself in us. A glance, a few spoken words are sufficient to tell us a story about a highly complex matter. We know that such impressions form with remarkable rapidity and with great ease. Subsequent observations may enrich or upset our view, but we can no more prevent its rapid growth than we can avoid perceiving a given visual object or hearing a melody'. These philosophical explorations have, in recent years received a wealth of empirical support. Eagly et al. (1991), for example, have shown that people believe that a person's judged attractiveness (their beauty) is positively related to their competence (both social and intellectual), adjustment, potency and general "goodness".

Much of the research on the neural bases of 'first impressions' has focused on initial appraisals of other people based on facial characteristics like attractiveness and perceived trustworthiness (for meta-analysis, see Mende-Siedlecki et al. 2011). First impressions based upon behavioral information have been extensively examined as well. This research has shown that our impressions of the people around us are powerfully influenced by the behaviors we come to associate with them (Todorov and Uleman 2002; Bliss-Moreau et al. 2008; Todorov and Olson 2008). Behavior-based impression formation can lead to automatic inferences regarding character traits (Todorov and Uleman 2003), and further, can be generalized to similar-looking others (Verosky and Todorov 2010). Typically, in such studies, people represented by faces paired with negative behavioral information are subsequently evaluated as being less trustworthy, and people paired with positive information are subsequently evaluated as being more trustworthy (Todorov and Olson 2008).

50 ms

Our ability to assess each other at a glance appears to be available to use when we are exposed to digital technology too. Lindgaard et al. (2006) conducted a series of studies to ascertain how quickly people form an appraisal of a web page's visual appeal. In a series of studies, participants rated the visual appeal of a series of web page. These pages had been previously rated for their visual appeal. In one study, a group of participants viewed the 25 highest-rated and 25 lowest-rated pages. While viewing each page for 500 ms, they assigned ratings to seven visual design characteristics. This established the reliability of visual appeal ratings and allowed the experimental team to select a subset of website home pages to use in the second study. The next study had two purposes—to determine the reliability of visual appeal ratings of the subset of 50 webpages and to begin to explore visual characteristics that may be related to visual appeal. However, of key interest is the final study which limited participants to view the pages for only 50 ms before asking them to rate their visual appeal. The researchers found ratings were highly correlated between the 50 and 500 ms conditions. Thus, visual appeal can be assessed within 50 ms, and it would be extremely unlikely that the means by which we make these assessments were different from those which evolution has provided us with the evaluate our fellow humans.

Personality and aesthetics

In the domain of interactive technologies, there is also substantial evidence that people often think of and treat interactive technology as though it was their friend, a pet or another person (e.g. Reeves and Nass 1996; Fogg and Nass 1997; Nass and Moon 2000) and ascribe a broad range of human attributes including personality to interactive technology (e.g. Brave et al. 2005; Johnson 2006, 2008).

Figure 4.1, for example, show two everyday artefacts which people reliably describe as serious, while other products are seen as extravert or playful. These judgements are typically made with the instruction, "imagine this xx were a person, what kind of person would it be" and to make the judgement on the basis of the product's appearance alone.

Govers and Mugge (2004) found that three of the "Big Five" personality dimensions, namely, extraversion, agreeableness and conscientiousness were found by to be salient to products, while Jordan 2002 had previously shown that consumers were able

Fig. 4.1 Two serious artefacts, image from Mugge et al. (2009) with permission from Elsevier

to rate photographs of vacuum cleaners, alarm clocks, kettles and toasters according to the Myers–Briggs Personality Indicator (Myers and McCaulley 1985) dimensions: extrovert/introvert; sensible/intuitive; thinking/feeling and judgmental/perceptive.

Astonishingly, consumers can both imagine and identify an *intuitive* vacuum cleaner. In a later small-scale study, Govers and Schoormans (2004) and her colleagues were able to design products with specific personality traits and have them recognised by laypeople, seventeen different dimensions—including authoritarian/liberal, bright/dim and conformist/rebel—were used to assign personalities to irons, shavers, shaver bags, epilators, air-cleaners, hair-dryers and coffee-makers.

Similarly, Govers et al. (2004) have suggested that respondents could attribute happiness, cuteness and toughness to drawings of domestic irons. And what demonstrates that this is not just whimsy, is that these attributions matched the personality traits intended by the product designers themselves no less.

Mugge et al. (2009) developed this approach further in the derivation of a product personality scale. Their work combined items from human personality scales with existing instruments from design and marketing studies designed to capture personality associations. These items were complemented by data from qualitative studies in which consumers were asked to describe a range of household products "as if they were a person". The final scale items (aloof, boring, cheerful, childish, cute, dominant, easy-going, honest, idiosyncratic, interesting, lively, modest, obtrusive, open, pretty, provocative, relaxed, serious, silly and untidy) were found to be reliable in the attribution of personality to pictures of cars and vacuum cleaners.

Designers have taken advantage of this to design products with specific personalities, for example, Govers et al. (2004) report that domestic irons designed by students to embody a range of personality traits were accurately recognised by respondents, while Desmet et al. (2008) established that devices intended to have a dominant, elegant or neutral (tangible) interaction style conveyed these traits effectively.

Product personality preference

The balance of evidence to date falls towards product preferences that mirror consumers' own personalities. Jordan's (1997) study suggests such a trend, based on participants' self-rating of their own personality. This is also evident in Govers and Mugge (2004), albeit using a 3rd party method where participants made judgements about the attachment of fictional consumers described in scenarios, to 'extrovert' and 'conscientious' toasters. Participants chose between statements such as "This toaster has no special meaning to John" and "This toaster is very dear to John".

The more extensive study reported by Govers and Schoormans (2005) investigates this tendency in greater depth. Forty-eight participants first imagined the personalities of each of several variants of screwdrivers, coffee-makers, soap-dispensers and wines with the invitation to make-believe and treat it "as if it were a person", then completed a questionnaire scale designed to capture the degree of perceived similarity between their own personality and that of the imagined "personality" of the product and lastly a scale capturing the perceived quality, desirability and attractiveness of the product. Products which were perceived to be similar to the participant's own personality were significantly preferred.

Personality and design qualities

Although there is rather less extant work which links personality traits with specific design qualities, one such study is reported by Brunel (2006), Brunel and Kumar (2007). In this instance participants rated a range of products represented in black-and-white photographs—automobiles, telephones, TVs and wall-clocks—against the five brand personality dimensions identified in Aaker (1997)—sincerity, excitement, competence, sophistication, and ruggedness, so far paralleling the procedure of many other studies. However, participants were also required to rate products against the aesthetic facets of recognition, simplicity, harmony, balance, unity, dynamics, timeliness/fashion, and novelty. A significant relationship was found between each of the personality dimensions and evaluations of aesthetic facets. Excitement, for example was related to timeliness and dynamism, while competence was associated with dynamism, unity and novelty.

Rasa

So far in this section we have focussed on judgements of attractiveness based on the face, while Lipp stressed the importance of the body as a whole, and here where better to introduce Indian erotic art. Ramachandran and Hirstein (1999) have developed a neurological theory of aesthetic experience with Ramachandran contributing his personal reflections on the carved stone female figures found in such art. Ramachandran writes of these figures in his *The Tell-Tale Brain* (2012) which he described as having shocked the British army when they first came across them in the 18th and 19th centuries. The figures are characterised by exaggerated female forms—large breasts, very narrow waists, and large hips like a modern-day self-promoting reality-show celebrity. (It is worth remembering that the British army came from a very repressed Victorian society which even covered the legs of pianos.)

Ramachandran and Hirstein seek to account for our interest and attraction to such bodily proportions in terms of peak shift. Suppose rats or pigeons are trained to respond to the presentation of rectangles, but not to squares (the animal will press a lever or peck a button on seeing a rectangle but ignore squares). Once trained, it has been observed that if these animals are presented a rectangle with exaggerated length (as compared to the original target rectangle), they will respond more vigorously to these new rectangles. It has been argued that squares and rectangles only differ along one dimension and if this is exaggerated, so too is the animal's response to it. This is the peak shift phenomenon. This peak shift also applies to the behaviour of seagull chicks which will peck for food at a stick with a red dot at the end (painted to resemble an adult gull's beak). The chicks will peck most at a stick with three red stripes. The stick only has one feature in common with an adult bird's beak and that is the red spot and that has been exaggerated.

Ramachandran and Hirstein claim that supporting evidence for this can be found in the research of Thornhill and Gangestad's (1999) into the attractiveness of artificially created faces. They found that woman (during periods of high fertility) prefer faces with exaggerated masculine features to average faces. Ramachandran and Hirstein compare this effect to the Sanskrit word "rasa," which they translate as "essence" and propose that an artist creating, say, a stone carving of a female extracts the rasa of the female body shape by exaggerating it in a direction that takes it away from the male body shape, and it is this which makes the sculpture more aesthetically pleasing. Example of this can also be found in the work of Alberto Vargas who is famous for his paintings of nudes and "pin-ups". Vargas was the creator of iconic World War-II era pin-ups for Esquire magazine known as "Varga Girls" which served to inspire the nose art of many American and allied World War II aircraft.[3]

4.6 Mood

Aesthetics and affect are closely linked, as in Norman's assertion that attractive things work better because if we are put in a good mood we are more likely to find them easily to use/enjoy using them/forgive them when they are troublesome. Here we first note briefly the work of Heidegger and Coyne on the subject of mood, then continue in a more applied vein to consider two genres of technique which, in very different ways, communicate mood, in one case by transporting people to worlds of the imagination and in the second by capturing the mood of design imagination.

Mood, emotion and imagining the sad park
Heidegger treats mood as an enduring state of being, in his terms Befindlichkeit, literally "how one finds oneself" or as "Richardson[4] (1963) puts it 'already-having-found-oneself-there-ness'. For Heidegger, we are necessarily in a mood of some sort, whether good, bad or one of supreme indifference. Moods help us make sense of our world. Coyne develops these concepts in the digital context in his 2016 publication

---

[3]https://www.pinterest.com/pin/357262182910501935/?nic=1.

[4]Richardson, W. J., 1963, Heidegger: Through Phenomenology to Thought, The Hague, Netherlands: Martinus Nijhoff Publishing.

Mood and Mobility, distinguishing persistent mood from ephemeral emotion. He further argues that digital products or media, whether through active use or more passive encounters, engender moods both in the individual and in the collective of media users, suggesting that the pervasive mood fostered by pervasive digital technology may be one of melancholy. Such observations bring to mind Philip K Dick's "Penfield mood organ" from Do Androids Dream of Electric Sheep (1968) which could induce any chosen mood in its user. And this in turn has been at least partially realised in those real-world digital technologies of more recent years which aim to influence mood by transporting their users to imaginary worlds. Here we should note that in contrast to the distinction just made between persistent mood and more ephemeral emotion, they are treated as synonyms in many reports of digital technology applications.

Among the more action-oriented video games of the early 1990s, Cyan World's more contemplative Myst, released in 1993, became the best-selling PC title for over a decade (McFarren 2012). Players used simple click and drag interactions to explore the game's world, visualised in (then) state-of-the-art graphic detail, through a series of puzzles. While the discovery of the stories behind the puzzles proved compulsive, what is noteworthy here is the powerful mood of engagement, relaxation and tranquillity intentionally engendered by the game and much remarked in gamer forums. In his interview with Myst's creators, Rand and Robyn Miller, McFarren reports how the music soundtrack played a major role in sustaining such a mood, despite Robyn Miller's doubts as to its effectiveness in the place of realistic sound effects. While Myst's purpose was ludic, the experience of imaginary worlds made possible by virtual environments have had serious applications in mood inducement in clinical settings. An early example of the genre is reported by Baños et al. (2004). Since VR applications had demonstrable potential in the clinical treatments of disorders of mood or emotion, the study aimed to investigate the interaction between emotion and the sense of presence—of being 'there'—in a virtual environment, in this case a simulated park. The researchers configured the park with the aim of inducing a mood of sadness, using a predominantly grey colour palette in the depiction of a cloudy day and leafless trees in a park devoid of other people, reinforced by sorrowful music. Results showed a positive relationship between the sense of presence and the emotional tone of the simulated environment. Research into mood regulation through engagement with imaginary virtual worlds continues, as, among many others, the review presented in Pizzoli et al. (2019) attests.

From a consideration of the place of imaginary virtual world in regulating moods, we now consider the crystallisation of design imagination in the form of moodboards (Fig. 4.2).

Moodboards convey the mood of a design through capturing and communicating the essence of the designer's imagination, predominantly in visual form. Many moodboards are crafted in physical form, but digital technologies also afford the capture and manipulation of elements in digital or mixed media format (Lucero and Martens 2005; Edward et al. 2009, among other examples). Godlewsky (2008) defines a moodboard as a collage implemented to introduce a certain mood, theme, or consumer world. Mood boards can be created with cutouts from various print products, or put together from sketches and photos. They are used in presentations to display as optimally as possible the designs that are to be presented. Creating mood boards at the beginning of a project can also help designers get in the right frame of mind for the task at hand, especially if the project requirements lie outside the designer's own experience. Or, in other words, where imagination is called upon. Here is a practising interior designer, Jenny Gibbs, interviewed in the Daily Telegraph newspaper. "Moodboards are a godsend. They're definitely not a step that should be skipped over. An interior is always a balancing act between imagination and practical considerations, and a visual collage is a great way to not only plan but also to check back and remind yourself of your original goals". (Fitzpatrick 2014).

Garner and McDonagh-Philp (2001) suggest that moodboards are "partly responses to an inner dialogue and partly provocation to become engaged in such a dialogue" and indeed the artefacts are essentially a resource for conversations, whether these are the Schön's designer in conversation with their materials, conversations among a design team, or designer-client conversations. The success in communicating mood or emotion to clients or users has been surprisingly little researched, but the study reported by Chang et al. (2014) does provide some indication that emotion may be accurately conveyed.

While their use is predominantly in the ideation phases of design, the empirical work with practicing designers reported in Lucero (2012) for example, identifies five roles for moodboards in design: framing of the problem; aligning stakeholder perspectives; paradoxing, which Lucero defines as "visually researching apparently conflicting or contradicting ideas"; abstracting, or "juxtaposing concrete and abstract imagery", and directing, by setting the future direction of the project. Lucero's 'paradoxing' is interesting here, since it appears to suggest the stimulation of new ways of seeing design concepts through contradiction, recalling Gurswitch (1964), for example, who describes imagination (understood in the sense of imagination as a source of imagery) as closely related to, or an extension of, perception thus giving rise to "seeing as". This kind of active perception account argues that the perceptual processes involved in imagery are the same processes active in perception enabling us to see things as they are or might be by discovering defining features.

4.7 Conclusion

This chapter has an inordinately long introduction. I'm afraid that was unavoidable. As we have seen, there is much more to aesthetics than mere appearance. Berger puts it you well when he writes, in Ways of Seeing (1972/2008), Berger wrote of 'the spectator-buyer [who] is meant … to imagine herself transformed by the product into an object of envy for others, an envy which will then justify loving herself'. We are no simple observers or admirers when it comes to aesthetics, we engage with the artefact by way of its aesthetics and through the power of our imaginations.

In conclusion, consider the following two "facts", one actual, the other make-believe. The real fact is that aesthetics is the most important factor in deciding which mobile phone to buy, in short, we buy on the basis of how it looks. The fictional

Coffee Shop

Fig. 4.2 Moodboard for coffee shop design (Wooten 2018, licensed under CC BY-SA 2.0)

fact is attributed to the ad-man, Donald Draper of the AMC TV series Mad Men where he tells us that "Advertising is based on one thing, happiness". A number of real-world admen have commented that this is a fair assessment and summary of their profession. Putting the two facts together, we might read this combination as, "buy this phone and it will make you happy" and this of course, is readily established in the purchaser's imagination.

References

Aaker J (1997) Dimensions of brand personality. J Mark Res 34(3):347–356

Asch S (1948) The psychology of ego-involvements: Social attitudes and identifications. Psychol Bull 45(2):165–171

Ballew CC II, Todorov A (2007) Predicting political elections from rapid and unreflective face judgments. PNAS 104(46):17948–17953

Baños RM, Botella C, Alcañiz M, Liaño V, Guerrero B, Rey B (2004) Immersion and emotion: their impact on the sense of presence. Cyberpsychol Behav 7(6):734–741

Bar M, Neta M, Linz H (2006) Very first impressions. Emotion 6(2):269

Beardsley MC (1969) Aesthetic experience regained. J Aesthet Art Crit 28:3–11

Bergeron V, Lopes DM (2012) Aesthetic theory and aesthetic science. Aesthetic science: Connecting minds, brains, and experience, 63

Berlyne DE (1974) Studies in the new experimental aesthetics. Wiley, New York

Berry DS (2000) Attractiveness, attraction, and sexual selection: evolutionary perspectives on the form and function of physical attractiveness. In: Zanna MP (ed) Advances in experimental social psychology. Academic, San Diego, pp 273–342

Bliss-Moreau E, Barrett LF, Wright CI (2008) Individual differences in learning the affective value of others under minimal conditions. Emotion 8(4):479

Bloch PH (1995) Seeking the ideal form: product design and consumer response. J Mark 59(3):16–29

Bloch PH, Brunel FF, Arnold TJ (2003) Individual differences in the centrality of visual product aesthetics: concept and measurement. J Consum Res 29(4):551–565

Borkenau P, Brecke S, Möttig C, Paelecke M (2009) Extraversion is accurately perceived after a 50-ms exposure to a face. J Res Pers 43:703–706

Brave S, Nass CI, Hutchinson K (2005) Computers that care: investigating the effects of orientation of emotion exhibited by an embodied computer agent. Int J Hum-Comput Stud 62(2):161–178

Brunel FF (2006) Design and the big five: linking visual product aesthetics to product personality. Boston University School of Management Working Paper

Brunel FF, Kumar R (2007) Design and the big five: linking visual product aesthetics to product personality. Adv Consum Res Assoc Consum Res 34:238–239

Brunner R, Emery S, Hall R (2009) How great products and services supply great user experiences. Pearson Education

Chang HM, Díaz M, Català A, Chen W, Rauterberg M (2014) Mood boards as a universal tool for investigating emotional experience. In: International conference of design, user experience, and usability. Cham, Springer, pp 220–231

Chatterjee A (2011) Neuroaesthetics: a coming of age story. J Cogn Neurosci 23(1):53–62

Chatterjee A, Vartanian O (2014) Neuroaesthetics. Trends Cogn Sci 18(7):370–375

Cinzia DD, Vittorio G (2009) Neuroaesthetics: a review. Curr Opin Neurobiol

Cuddy AJC, Fiske ST, Glick P (2008) Warmth and competence as universal dimensions of social perception: the stereotype content model and the BIAS map. In: Zanna MP (ed) Advances in experimental social psychology, vol 40. Academic, New York, pp 61–149

Cunningham MR (1986) Measuring the physical in physical attractiveness: quasi-experiments on the sociobiology of female facial beauty. J Pers Soc Psychol 50:925–935

Desmet PMA, Nicolás JCO, Schoormans JP (2008) Product personality in physical interaction. Des Stud 29:458–477

Dutton D (2009) The art instinct: beauty, pleasure, & human evolution. Oxford University Press, Oxford

Eagly AH, Ashmore RD, Makhijani MG, Longo LC (1991) What is beautiful is good, but…: A meta-analytic review of research on the physical attractiveness stereotype. Psychol Bull 110(1):109

Edward A, Fadzli S, Setchi R (2009) Comparative study of developing physical and digital mood boards. In: Anais (ed) 5th international conference on innovative production machines and systems, Carfiff, UK

Fitzpatrick M (2014) Interiors: use a mood board to pin down the right look. www.telegraph.co.uk/lifestyle/interiors/10599142/Interiors-use-a-mood-board-to-pin-down-the-right-look.html. Accessed 2019 Oct

Fogg BJ, Nass C (1997) Silicon sycophants: the effects of computers that flatter. Int J Hum-Comput Stud 46:551–561

Garner S, McDonagh-Philp D (2001) Problem interpretation and resolution via visual stimuli: the use of 'mood boards' in design education. J Art Des Educ 20(1):57

Godlewsky T (2008) Mood Board. In: Erlhoff M, Marshall T (eds) Design dictionary. Board of international research in design. Birkhäuser, Basel

Gombrich EHJ (1963) Meditations on a hobby horse and other essays on the theory of art. Phaidon, London

Govers PC, Mugge R (2004) I love my Jeep, because its tough like me: The effect of product-personality congruence on product attachment. In: Proceedings of the fourth international conference on design and emotion, Ankara, Turkey, pp 12–14

Govers PCM, Schoormans JPL (2004) Product personality and its influence on consumer preference. J Consum Mark 22(4):189–197

Govers PC, Schoormans JP (2005) Product personality and its influence on consumer preference. J Consum Mark

Govers PCM, Hekkert P, Schoormans JPL (2004) Happy, cute and tough: can designers create a product personality that consumers understand? In: MacDonagh D, Hekkert P, Van Erp J, Gyi D (eds) Design and emotion, the experience of everyday things. Taylor & Francis, London, pp 345–349

Gurswitch A (1964, 1st ed.) The field of consciousness, vol. 2. Duquesne University Press, Pittsburgh, PA

Hallnäs L, Redström J (2002) From use to presence: on the expressions and aesthetics of everyday computational things. ACM Trans Comput Hum Inter 9(2):106–124

Hassenzahl M (2004) Beauty, goodness & usability in inter products. HCI 19:319–349

Hassenzahl M (2008) Aesthetics in interactive products: correlates and consequences of beauty. In: Schifferstein H, Hekkert P (eds) Product experience. Elsevier, San Diego, pp 287–302

Johnson RD, Marakas GM, Palmer JW (2006) Differential social attributions toward computing technology: An empirical investigation. Int J Hum Comput Stud 64(5):446–460

Johnson RD, Veltri NF, Hornik S (2008) Attributions of responsibility toward computing technology: The role of interface social cues and user gender. Int J Hum Comput Int 24(6):595–612

Jordan PW (1997) Products as personalities. In: Robertson SA (ed) Contemporary ergonomics. Taylor & Francis, London, pp 73–78

Jordan PW (2002) The personalities of products. In: Green WS, Jordan PW (eds) Pleasure with products: beyond usability. Taylor & Francis, London, pp 19–48

Khaslavsky J, Shedroff N (1999) Understanding the seductive experience. Commun ACM 42(5):45–49

Kuroso M, Kashimura K (1995) Apparent usability vs. inherent usability, CHI'95 Conference Companion. In: Conference on human factors in computing systems, Denver, Colorado, pp 292–293

Lavie T, Tractinsky N (2004) Assessing dimensions of perceived visual aesthetics of web sites. Int J Hum Comput Stud 60(3):269–298

Leder H, Nadal M (2014) Ten years of a model of aesthetic appreciation and aesthetic judgments: The aesthetic episode–Developments and challenges in empirical aesthetics. Br J Psychol 105(4):443–464

Leder H, Belke B, Oeberst A, Augustin D (2004) A model of aesthetic appreciation and aesthetic judgments. Br J Psychol 95(4):489–508

Levinson J (1996) The pleasures of aesthetics. Cornell University Press, Ithaca

Lindgaard G, Fernandes G, Dudek C, Brown J (2006) Attention web designers: you have 50 milliseconds to make a good first impression! Behav Infor Technol 25(2):115–126

Lucero A (2012) Framing, aligning, paradoxing, abstracting, and directing: how design mood boards work. In: Proceedings of the designing interactive systems conference, ACM, pp 438–447

Lucero A, Martens JBOS (2005) Mood Boards: Industrial designers' perception of using mixed reality. In: Proceedings of SIGCHI NL Conference, pp 13–16

MacLean PD (1990) The triune brain in evolution: role in paleocerebral functions. Springer Science & Business Media, Berlin

Martin CL (1998) Relationship marketing: a high-involvement product attribute approach. J Prod Brand Manage

McFarren D (2012) The making of myst http://www.nintendolife.com/news/2012/11/feature_the_making_of_myst. Accessed 2019 Oct

Mende-Siedlecki P, Kober H, Ochsner KN (2011) Emotion regulation: neural bases. The Oxford handbook of social neuroscience, vol 277; Mende-Siedlecki P, Cai Y, Todorov A (2012) The neural dynamics of updating person impressions. Soc Cogn Affect Neurosci 8(6):623–631

Mende-Siedlecki P, Baron SG, Todorov A (2013) Diagnostic value underlies asymmetric updating of impressions in the morality and ability domains. J Neurosci 33(50):19406–19415

Mugge R, Govers PC, Schoormans JP (2009) The development and testing of a product personality scale. Des Stud 30(3):287–302

Myers IB, McCaulley MH (1985) Manual; a guide to the development and use of the Myers-Briggs type indicator, 5th edn. Consulting Psychologists Press, Palo Alto

Nass C, Moon Y (2000) Machines and mindlessness: social responses to computers. J Soc Issues 56(1):81–103

Norman DA (2004) Ad-hoc personas & empathetic focus. http://jnd.org/dn.mss/ad-hoc_personas_empathetic_focus.html. Accessed 11 Mar 2010

Olson IR, Marshuetz C (2005) Facial attractiveness is appraised in a glance. Emotion 5(4):498

Petersen MG, Iversen OS, Krogh PG, Ludvigsen M (2004) Aesthetic interaction: a pragmatist's aesthetics of interactive systems. In: Proceedings of the 5th conference on designing interactive systems: processes, practices, methods, and techniques, pp 269–276

Petersen MG, Hallnäs L, Jacob RJK (eds.) (2008) Special issue on aesthetic interaction. ACM Trans Comput Hum Inter 15(3–4)

Pizzoli SFM, Mazzocco K, Tribertx S, Monzani D, Raya MLA, Pravettoni G (2019) User-centered virtual reality for promoting relaxation: an innovative approach. Front Psychol 10:479

Ramachandran VS, Hirstein W (1999) The science of art: a neurological theory of aesthetic experience. J Conscious Stud 6(6–7):15–51

Redström J (2008) Tangled interaction: on the expressiveness of tangible user interfaces. ACM Trans Comput Hum Inter 15(4):1–17

Reeves B, Nass C (1996) The media equation: how people treat computers, television and new media like real people and places. Cambridge University Press, Cambridge

Reimann M, Zaichkowsky J, Neuhaus C, Bender T, Weber B (2010) Aesthetic package design: a behavioral, neural, and psychological investigation. J Consum Psychol 20(4):431–441

Rule NO, Ambady N (2008) Brief exposures: Male sexual orientation is accurately perceived at 50 ms. J Exp Soc Psychol 44:1100–1105

Russo B, de Moraes A (2003) The lack of usability in design icons: an affective case study about Juicy Salif. In: Proceedings of the 2003 international conference on designing pleasurable products and interfaces, pp 146–147

Santayana G (1896/1955) The sense of beauty: being the outline of aesthetic theory, vol 238. Courier Corporation

Scheib JE, Gangestad SW, Thornhill R (1999) Facial attractiveness, symmetry and cues of good genes. In: Proceedings of the royal society of London. series B: biological sciences, vol 266(1431), pp 1913–1917

Shusterman R (1992) Pragmatist aesthetics: living beauty. Rethinking Art 2:45

Stolnitz J (1969) Aesthetics and the philosophy of art criticism (reprinted in introductory readings in aesthetics. John Hospers (ed). The Free Press, New York, p 27

Thornhill R, Gangestad SW (1993) Human facial beauty Hum Nat 4(3):237–269

Thornhill R, Gangestad SW (1999) Facial attractiveness. Trends Cogn Sci 3(12):452–460

Todorov A, Olson IR (2008) Robust learning of affective trait associations with faces when the hippocampus is damaged, but not when the amygdala and temporal pole are damaged. Soc Cogn Affect Neurosci 3(3):195–203

Todorov A, Uleman JS (2002) Spontaneous trait inferences are bound to actors' faces: Evidence from a false recognition paradigm. J Person Soc Psychol 83(5):1051

Todorov A, Uleman JS (2003) The efficiency of binding spontaneous trait inferences to actors' faces. J Exp Soc Psychol 39(6):549–562

Todorov A, Pakrashi M, Oosterhof NN (2009) Evaluating faces on trustworthiness after minimal time exposure. Soc Cogn 27(6):813–833

Udsen LE, Jørgensen AH (2005) The aesthetic turn: unravelling recent aesthetic approaches to human-computer interaction. Digital Creativity 16(04):205–216

Ulrich KT (2006) Design: creation of artifacts in society, "Aesthetics in Design". Pontifica Press

Van der Laan LN, De Ridder DT, Viergever MA, Smeets PA (2012) Appearance matters: neural correlates of food choice and packaging aesthetics. PloS One 7(7)

Verosky SC, Todorov A (2010) Generalization of affective learning about faces to perceptually similar faces. Psychol Sci 21(6):779–785

Walton KL (1993) Metaphor and prop oriented make-believe. Eur J Philos 1(1):39–57

Weiser M (1999) The computer for the 21st century. ACM SIGMOBILE Mobile Comput Commun Rev 3(3):3–11

Willis J, Todorov A (2006) First impressions: making up your mind after a 100-ms exposure to a face. Psychol Sci 17(7): 592–598

Wooten, P (2018) Coffeeshop moodboard. Image available at https://www.flickr.com/photos/paul_wooten/39979655632/in/photolist-23USbKs

Zolli A (2004) Why design matters more. Am Demogr 26:52–55

Chapter 5
Imaginary Use

Chapter Thumbnail

We have been using tools and technology to achieve our goals for millions of years, reaching back from the earliest tools of stone or wood or bone artefacts to the latest 3D printed parts or microfabricated semiconductor. Our use of these tools is based, in part, on our ability to formulate a goal and to imagine a technological solution (that is, tools plus appropriate skills). However, since the advent of digital technology, use has changed. Once we would have picked up an axe and swung it, chopping wood for home and hearth, now we use tools *indirectly* via a user interface. We pick up our phones and tap an icon—a little picture—which we are invited to make-believe stands for access to a service, or contact with other people, or the world as a whole including someone else who will chop and deliver logs for us. In using digital technology, the importance of our imaginations has become paramount.

This chapter identifies the interplay between use and imagination in a number of ways. Firstly, most digital technology which is used by people is either the result of a prototyping approach or a methodology which employs prototyping. A prototype is an early, unfinished version of the target technology and is frequently used during its development on the basis of pretence. Users of prototypes agree to make-believe its use, is to a greater or less extent, close enough to the finished (or next) version. This is particular true of low-fidelity prototypes. Secondly, our use of digital technology is indirect as it relies on an interface of some kind. Very many (and possibly most) user interfaces rely on the metaphorical portrayal of the technology and in turn, metaphor relies unequivocally on imagination. Next, our experience with digital technology (according to the ISO definition at least) includes imaginary use. Here, experience is thought to be the product of anticipated or expected or the imagined use of technology, which does not, of course, require the involvement of technology itself. Then there are those technologies which are expressly imaginary. We end this chapter with a discussion of VR and wonder why there is no mention of imagination or make-believe in the various accounts of it.

© Springer Nature Switzerland AG 2020
P. Turner, *Imagination + Technology*, Human–Computer Interaction Series,
https://doi.org/10.1007/978-3-030-37348-1_5

5.1   Introduction

a key problem for neuroscience is to explain how matter becomes imagination
Modell (2003, p. 1)

This chapter is concerned with the interplay between imagination and making-believe and the use of digital technology. We have identified four different ways in which these can be observed, these are:

i.   The use of prototypes within HCI;
ii.   The use of metaphor at the user interface. We say again, metaphor is understood, not as a literary device but literal one, involving a transfer, with one thing standing for another;
iii. The imaginary use of technology including how we might expect to use the technology in the future and how we have used it in the past.
iv.   Imaginary user interfaces, and imaginary objects of interaction.

And we conclude with a meditation on the astonishing absence of any mention of make-believe or imagination in virtual reality.

5.2   Prototyping

It is difficult to exaggerate the importance of prototypes and prototyping to the design, speculative thinking and evaluation processes of human computer interaction and digital product design. Indeed, the most common form of make-believe within HCI must be the creation and use of a prototype of the target system, inevitably prototypes of all kinds are an intrinsic part of the design and development processes.

A prototype has been defined in a number of ways and even the question of what a prototype actually prototypes has been posed too (Houde and Hill 1997). We are told, for example, that a prototype approximates to the finished version although we might be hard pressed to understand what constitutes a "finished version". For example, I am currently using version 16.16.15 of Microsoft Word for Mac; more than 30 years ago I was using v1.x; and in coming years I expect to continue to be a loyal customer. Exactly what we mean by a *finished product* is clearly a matter of debate, definition and marketing policy and given the frequency of software releases, it remains somewhat elusive.

One of the earliest forms of prototyping used in HCI was low fidelity, paper prototyping. This technique dates from a time when prototyping an interactive system was an arduous process which involved writing lines and lines of code just to draw a simple shape on a screen. Paper prototyping was devised as means of mocking up and evaluating an early interface design using paper, cardboard, and fragments of plastic sheeting to simulate windows and other bits and bobs. A user was then recruited who is then asked to step through a typical interaction with the system. (This process bears a number of similarities with the Wizard of Oz technique described above and these two different methods are often conflated and confused). The designer pretends to be the computer and he or she physically manages the interaction with the make-believe system. In practice, the participants in these design sessions play act, role play (or as we prefer) make-believe that the prototype they are using will more-or-less behave just like the real thing (e.g. Snyder 2003).

Role playing with prototypes

Prototypes are tried out, experimented with and perhaps more than anything else are played with, often with individuals playing specific roles. The earliest recorded use of role playing and low-fidelity prototyping in the design of computer systems dates back to the UTOPIA project of the 1980s (Ehn 1988). Since then the technique has been rediscovered, refined and tweaked and re-applied by successive generations. For example, Binder (1999) reports on the use of in situ role playing with low-fi prototypes as a way of involving workers in the design of a PDA-based[1] system in an industrial setting. It has also been used to explore specific phases of product development, for example, Kuutti et al. (2002) have described the use of prototypes and role playing in concept generation, and Boess et al. (2007) have made the case for a similar approach in design concept ideation. While Howard et al. (2002) used professional actors to act out scenarios of mobile computing and Salvador and Sato (1999) developed "Focus Troupe" as a way of using drama to get feedback from potential customers on new product ideas and Buchenau and Fulton Suri (2000) describe "Experience Prototyping" as the use of role playing and low-fi prototypes for exploring design concepts. And Howard et al. (2002) have reported a form of scenario-based design that aims to increase stakeholders' sense of 'immersion' in the happenings and situations depicted in the scenarios. In their approach, scenarios are 'acted out' by actors and/or candidate users during participatory design sessions, rather than being 'walked through' by designers and users. In usage, the scenarios play a role similar to stage directions in theatrical performance. Props are a vital accompaniment to such scenarios. Props, as ever focus and direct the attention of the design team and stakeholders during participatory design sessions. Experience from the prior use of role-playing has shown that little training is needed to be able to do this. The simplest explanation for this being that they are playing, and play is a basic skill that acquire during childhood. Goffman (1978) in his "The Presentation of Self in Everyday Life" argued that drama is the best metaphor for everyday social life, and that we all play roles most of the time. Central to role playing and play, as to drama and performing arts, is the "as-if". By letting people and objects represent something else, we create an imagined world within the real world.

How was it for you?

From a practical perspective however, prototypes are props. They can be used to initiate and mediate conversations with project stakeholders or (reflexively) with the designer. Our interest is, of course, their interaction with imagination/make-believe. So, let us suppose that we have created stable versions of an app and want to know

---

[1]Personal digital assistants were, a generation ago, popular tablet computers.

about its usability or aesthetics or how much people might pay to use it. In such circumstances, we would a recruit a cohort of participants and provide them with the prototype, and then ask them to complete a task designed to reveal the answer to the evaluators' question. The participants would be asked, in a variety of different ways, "how was it?". The task varies by technology and the wording of the "how was it" question varies as a consequence of the question we wish to ask. In essence, participants are asked, in what is a "debriefing stage" to remember/re-experience the relevant details from their experience.

Here we must insert a caveat, however as there is a growing body of literature which shows that imagining experiences which did not occur can change memory. Empirical studies have shown that when people think about or imagine something which did not happen, a so-called "a false event", a corresponding false memory can be established. This imagination inflation can occur in the absence of overt social pressure, and when hypothetical events are imagined only briefly. Overall, studies of imagination inflation show that imagining a counter-factual event can make people more confident that it actually occurred. "Imagination inflation" (e.g. Garry et al. 1996; Goff and Roediger 1998), can be observed when imagining an event can cause someone to "remember" having experienced it. But it is not all bad, as we note that Joyce (2003) writes that, we know what an experience is like if we can imagine it correctly, and we will do so if we recognise the experience as it is imagined. Joyce identifies a constraint on adequate accounts of how we ordinarily imagine experiences correctly: the capacities to imagine and to recognise the experience must be jointly operative at the point of forming an intention to imagine the experience.

5.3 The Metaphorical Use of Technology

All software applications are used indirectly. They required a user interface which in turn comprises a picture on a screen, a keyboard and a mouse. That picture is usually a collage of familiar representations like scissors, coloured marker pens, erasers, paint-pots, or are small pictures themselves (e.g. clocks, clouds, footballs, pieces of fruit, cameras or trashcans) or even single letters (e.g. "f" or "g" which prompt us to remember one some global software superpower), and the background to this is "wallpaper" (which explains the decorating analogy) or a "desktop". We recognise these symbols as conventions, or as objects offering pseudo-affordances or "perceived affordances" but, more simply, they are standing as metaphors. To make sense of them involves our semantic memory (what does it mean), our procedural memories (which keystrokes and menu items) and our episodic memories ("I remember doing this last week") and our imaginations. A user interface embodies possibilities, frozen imaginary states, if you like.

This has changed, of course, now we now tap, swipe (up and down, and side to side), and we pinch and stretch (is that the word) those little pictures. Logically, of course, this is no different yet despite being still described (in certain quarters) as "direct manipulation", but it is not, it is metaphorical.

Tognazzini (1991), an influential designer at Apple™, has offered the more general suggestion that communicating the underlying structure and operation of an interactive system is best achieved by means of a metaphor or analogy. This can be realised by using a set of objects (such as elements of the user interface) which can activate a metaphorical or analogical connection to the real world. Having made this connection, the user of the system can anticipate its behaviour. Further, Lakoff and Johnson (1980) have argued that metaphor and analogy are the very bases of our cognition and these ideas have been developed further by Fauconnier and Turner (2003) who have argued that all learning and all thinking consist of blends of metaphors based on simple bodily experiences.

Carroll and Mack (1985) describe metaphors as 'seeds' or 'kernels' which stimulate associations and lead to the formation of mental models. They also discuss the embedded quality of self-generated metaphors in learning. These self-generated metaphors have been found to be treated as 'givens' and accepted unconditionally by learners, whereas metaphors that are taught to learners have been found to be ineffective (1985). Furthermore, Halasz and Moran (1982) have argued that the use of metaphor in the design of interactive systems is harmful because firstly, computers offer functionality which do not correspond naturally to their real-world analogues (they suggest that a computer filing cabinet does behave like its real counterpart but the idea of password protected file access has no natural equivalent). Secondly, there are times when we intend to convey a point, not a whole system of thought (a computer desktop is a surface on which lie tools and documents but is not made from wood nor can be stood upon to change a light fitting).

Marcus (1994), in discussing the range of metaphors commonly used, notes that these can be divided into nouns (e.g. desks, books, photographs, disks) and verbs (move, flow, select, create) but, of course, when discussing the Web spatial metaphors dominate. The Web is conceived as space—a cyber-space which we are said to navigate and in which those less familiar can become lost. But the Web is not a space, it is not res extensa: it is a distributed application running on the Internet.

Finally, it might have been also noticed that most of the references to metaphor and interactive systems are quite old (most of them are mid 1980s). It has been 40 years since metaphor was an important design issue in HCI, since then the desktop has become a convention; an on-screen 'toolbox' merely the name of that interface widget. So, why has metaphor persisted? Modell (2003, p.25) tells us that, "… the source of the imagination, what makes us uniquely human, is an unconscious metaphoric process". This makes imagination embodied.

5.4 The Imaginary Experience of Technology

The very idea of imaginary user experience (UX) being something worthy of our consideration sounds vaguely contradictory. Researching or thinking about user experience is (surely) by definition concerned with the results of someone using digital technology and anything else, is just not the case. Except of course, for the small matter of the formal ISO (2009) definition of UX including the line: "*person's per-ceptions and responses that result from the use and/or anticipated use of a system, product or service*".

Describing UX as "perceptions and responses" resulting from use makes this squarely psychological and clearly common-sensical. We can measure both percep-tions and responses and these can be used as a part of an evaluation telling us whether product A is preferred/easier to use/is more fun to use (and so forth) than product B. Commercial decisions can be made on the basis of such data. But the reference to "anticipated use" goes beyond this. Anticipated use refers to planning to use or making-believe the use of the digital product ("perhaps in one's mind's eye") or imagining oneself "showing it off" at a party, travelling to work, or even in a hurry. We can imagine a situation where we ask people to imagine wearing, say a smart watch and then to anticipate how they might use it or feel about it. We can ask, "if you are planning to buy a smart watch, which of these (say) three watches would you choose?". We can imagine presenting people with a tray of watches or a series of photographs or simple prototypes. The product need not be present—a situation which is almost entirely the case when working with low fidelity or early prototypes. This is user experience without the experience or the technology—just the user and their imagination.

Every user experience relies on an appraisal, such as, "was it fun?", "is it pleasing on the eye?", "will it do the job?" but to understand this is to recognise that these user experiences have two components. They are composed of real-world events and interactions and possible, plausible events and interactions. More specifically, UX comprises the experiences of using the technology here and now and wondering whether it can be used on the move or with friends or later this evening. This reflects the make-up of our everyday lives. We do live not solely in the present but in a melange of what-ifs, maybes, day-dreams and fantasies. UX comprises this mix of the actual and possible, the actual and the imagined.

The ISO definition of UX
The wording of ISO standard has also been amplified for clarification and comes with the following notes (the italics are mine):

Note 1: User experience includes the user's emotions, beliefs, preferences, percep-tions, physical and psychological responses, behaviours and accomplishments that occur *before*, during and after use.
Note 2: User experience is a consequence of brand image, presentation, functionality, system performance, interactive behaviour, and assistive capabilities of a system, product or service. It also results from the user's internal and physical state resulting from prior experiences, attitudes, skills and personality; and from the context of use.
Note 3: Usability, when interpreted from the perspective of *the users' personal goals*, can include the kind of perceptual and emotional aspects typically associated with user experience. Usability criteria can be established so as to assess aspects of user experience.

In note 1, we have the explicit inclusion of the user's response *before* use. Then again in note 3, we are asked to adopt the perspective of the users' personal goals, what if thinking.

5.5 Imaginary User Interfaces, and Imaginary Objects of Interaction

This review—inevitably a partial snapshot—of imaginative, speculative but potentially realisable technologies, focusses on the invisible or immaterial yet, in some sense, tangible.

Work by Fishkin et al. (1998) recognises that there have been a number of examples of user interfaces created which have removed the barrier between the user interface per se and the computation device being used. These new interfaces have the user physically manipulating the computational device directly itself rather than, say, a graphical interface with pictures mediating our use. These examples, which we would now recognise as tangible user interfaces, however can also be seen as a step on the path to leading towards (what they describe as) the ideal of an invisible user interface.

However, it was Gustafson et al. (2010) who fully established the concept of "imaginary user interfaces" and demonstrated a mid-air non-visual interaction technique: once the origin of the imaginary space is defined, users could point and draw freely in that space. Thus "imaginary interfaces," are spatial user interfaces, in which objects are selected by pointing at them directly, without the mediation of a screen. Gustafson et al. (2011) subsequently explored imaginary interactions with a smartphone by mapping its home screen to locations on the user's palm; a camera tracked users' pointing at locations on the palm, the touch events being then sent wirelessly to a physical iPhone. Experiments showed that participants, drawing on spatial memory of their phone layout, could transfer this knowledge to the palm interface and were able to recall 61% of the home screen icons on their smartphones and to reliably target those icons on the palm. A later, detailed investigation (Gustafson et al. 2013) provided a more thorough understanding of palm-based interaction, as shown in Fig. 5.1 by highlighting the relationship between tactile cues in the palm and the imaginary user interface.

The same principle was employed for "PalmRC," a system designed to replace the TV remote control with the palm of the hand (Dezfuli et al. 2012), while Steins et al. (2013) evaluated imaginary interfaces for mimicking input on various devices, such as a steering wheel or a joystick. In parallel developments, Kumar and Pandithurai (2013) describe the Sixth Sense prototype where a wearable pendant containing a small projector, mirror and camera connects to a mobile device in the user's pocket. The ensemble allows visual information to be projected on physical objects to be used as interfaces, which in turn provides an interface for gesture-based interaction, thereby bridging "the gap between the physical world and the digital world, bringing

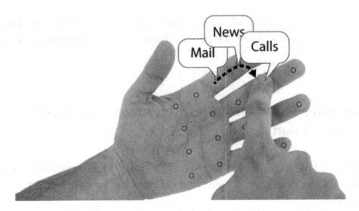

Fig. 5.1 Palm based imaginary interface to a phone (Gustafson et al. 2013, image by kind permission Patrick Baudisch)

intangible, digital information out into the tangible world, and allowing us to interact with this information via natural hand gestures." The authors further suggest that the technology could be integrated with voice recognition.

Imaginary interfaces have also been successfully applied in prototype form to smart environments with multiple remote displays or involving multiple users (Rateau et al. 2014) and there is also clearly huge potential from this family of technologies for ludic applications (Gustafson et al. 2013) as illustrated in Fig. 5.2.

Since a virtual or augmented environment may contain remote objects with which the user may wish to interact, various strategies for the ergonomic optimization of mid-air interactions have also been proposed (Montano Murillo et al. 2017). The possibilities for interaction with the imaginary and the unseen continue to expand, one recent focus being the ability to interact with apparently empty space in mid-air, exemplified by Schipor and Vatavu (2018), who present and empirical investigation of the potential for 'pinning' information mid-air in user space, together with a handy set of practitioner guidelines for others in the field, and Popovici et al. (2019)

Fig. 5.2 VR imaginary basketball: there is no visible ball; players get information from watching each other and a small amount of auditory feedback (Gustafson et al. 2013, image by kind permission Patrick Baudisch)

who demonstrate TV control through mid-air pointing. Contactless haptic interaction and feedback are also now available. The UltraHaptics technology (Carter et al. 2013) affords haptic feedback above interactive surfaces, using ultrasound to project focussed sensations onto users' hands. In turn this offers opportunities for the development of more controlled gesture-based interaction, the provision of information in a haptic layer—the example is cited of a heat map to indicate population density as the hand hovers over a map—and the operation of controls in visually restricted displays.

Interacting with holographic projections
A body of recent work has extended developments in haptics in combination with holographic technology to endow holograms with tangible feedback, thus enhancing their perceived presence (Kergevant et al. 2017) and for potential use in a variety of digital signage applications, such as that reported in Limerick et al. (2019).

Holographic projections, placed in a user's real space, can be walked 'around', 'moved' or 'interacted' with directly. The quote marks here are because, of course, such actions are imaginary—there is no physical subject of 'interaction'. Bach et al. (2017) for example, evaluate the efficacy of an AR head-mounted display which produces interactive, 'tangible' holographic projections of 3D scatterplot visualisations into a user's real world. As compared to handheld tablet and desktop supported interactions, holographic interaction performed well on visualisation tasks that required spatial perception and interactions with a high degree of freedom, but less successfully where precision and speed were required. Unsurprisingly, perhaps, users rated the holographic condition as low on familiarity and high on the physical effort required. Such perceived unfamiliarity of interaction can be ameliorated if the users' hands are rendered visible in the virtual space, as demonstrated in a prototype reported in Funk et al. (2017).

Real-world applications proposed most commonly comprise, ludic, data visualisation or cultural heritage applications, while Kim et al. (2019) report a prototype demonstration that provides interactive holograms of consumer goods, thus of affording "a memorable in-store experience with the merging of digital and physical interactions". Among the many projects in the cultural heritage arena (a recent review may be found in Bekele and Champion 2019), perhaps the most noteworthy in the current context is that discussed by Pedersen and her colleagues (2017). The Tomb-Seer application is designed to complement a physical, life-size exhibit reproducing an Egyptian tomb, which invites visitors to "stand inside the tomb and imagine an ancient lifestyle, to imagine another time". TombSeer presents a 3D holographic, AR interface to virtual, historical artefacts such as a funerary urn. Users are able to 'stare' to select such an object, grab, pick up or move it, among other actions, and thereby to "create the feeling of *being there* in a historic space, by moving around and engaging with the exhibit in a more immersive way, and imagining the lives of the people who would have gone to the tomb." Not only is the interaction imaginary, but so too is the experience thus afforded.

Araujo et al.'s Snake Charmer (2016) employs robotic arms in support of lending physical characteristics to holographic objects, with the aim of avoiding the situation where "one has but to reach out and grasp nothing but air to destroy the suspension of disbelief". Signer and Curtin (2017) also propose the enhancement of mobile, tangible holograms in mixed reality with physical properties such as texture and temperature in environments where users can move around freely, experience haptic feedback and collaborate with others to manipulate the shape of such holograms, through the use of "special glasses which will not only augment the user's view of the physical environment with the necessary digital holograms but also offer the possibility to track the spatial layout of the environment as well as any physical objects via depth and environmental cameras" and the donning of a pair of robotic arms each of which has "a sphere which is used to capture the input from as user's hand or finger but also serves as an output device for different physical features." Application scenarios in automotive design and interior design are suggested.

5.6 And, of Course, Virtual Reality

Virtual reality has been with us since the 1960s and from these early beginnings has promised us so much. Truth be said, the current state of virtual reality technology is very impressive. It has delivered on the promise of home VR powered by games consoles; similarly, for commercial training applications (e.g. aerospace, firefighting, and so forth); and in other specialist areas (e.g. industrial design) and as a form of artistic expression and in medicine and other therapeutic application. At the same time, a number of major users (or perhaps we should say, corporate users in particular) have expressed misgivings about the maturity of the technology (e.g. BBC, google) and have recently abandoned VR projects.

Our interest here is not so much the technology's computational ability to draw n polygons per second, but on the experience it offers the user. While there is abundant evidence that VR can serve as an excellent platform for training and in medicine and gaming but what of the "being somewhere else aspect of VR"? Putting on a head mounted display (HMD) and starting the virtual reality software promises to take us to the flight-deck of a commercial airliner, or scalpel in hand, drop us into an operating theatre, or as part of an interactive display in the museum allow us to walk round the reconstruction of a roman villa. These instances all offer the user the distinguishing features of this technology which is a sense of immersion or tele-presence in the aircraft, surgical unit or villa.

However, in reporting the creation, design and evaluation of these virtual environments their authors do so without reference to either imagination or make-believe. But what is even more curious is that, describing our experience of a virtual reality game (using recognisably similar technology to the commercial or "serious" applications of VR) as make-believe would be quite legitimate.

Immersion and presence

It has not always been this way as Burdea and Coiffet (1994) have observed that virtual reality is both interactive and immersive and specifically requires a place for imagination. Bearing in mind that they were writing more than a quarter century ago, the role of imagination, they proposed, is to make up for the short fall in the technology—they note that, *"the extent to which an application is able to solve a particular problem, that is, the extent to which a simulation performs well, depends therefore very much on the human imagination"*. In this context, they treat imagination as the mind's capacity to perceive non-existent things. For these writers, imagination fills in the gaps (makes up for any shortcomings in the technology's ability to create a virtual environment). In parallel with this, presence appeared as an academic discipline, with the publication of the first journal dedicated to its research. This is not to suggest, however, that designers, artists and writers have been unaware of the power of their media to create a sense of immersion or transportation or feelings of being present elsewhere, from long before this time. Prehistoric cave art may have been created for this very purpose and the use of stained glass in churches and cathedrals has been recognised as a means of transporting church-goers to higher, spiritual dimensions. Indeed, stories of all kinds, irrespective of medium, have this power to transport, immerse, engage and to create a sense of being other than where we currently are. The English romantic poet Samuel Taylor Coleridge coined the term, *"the willing suspension of disbelief"* to describe the apparent willingness of readers to engage with stories irrespective of their credibility. Though we are mindful of the earlier and more sober observations of the David Hume who wrote of *imaginative resistance*, that is, the reluctance we feel when we are invited to embrace something unbelievable. Unhappily, the expression the willing suspension of disbelief is now being used was as little thought as similar slogans such as "user friendly".

So, before considering what others have defined as presence, just what is our central question? It is this, what is it that a cave painting, a stained-glass window, a poem and a myriad of digital technology have in common? A tempting answer might lie with inverting Coleridge's "the willing suspension of disbelief" from a double-negative to the positive statement, "the willingness to believe". However even if we emphasize the temporary nature of this belief, *belief*, in itself, is much too powerful a claim. When we watch a (fictional) movie we do not believe what we see, nor do we suspend disbelief instead *we act (think and feel) as though* what we are engaged with were the case.

So, returning to the examples we have already considered, we do not propose that the people who first gazed on cave paintings actually believed themselves to be in the presence of aurochs nor, while in churches, to be in the company of spiritual beings. Neither do we propose that people believe themselves transported to a "stately pleasure dome" after reading Kublai Khan nor fighting aliens on the surface of Mars with their space marine buddies in a games arcade. What we *do* propose is that people readily act, think, react and emote as though we were or might be in these situations.

This "as-if", "as-though" and "might be" indirection is one of the key differences between believing and making-believe. So rather than believing that we are elsewhere, we propose that we make-believe that we are.

The power of make-believe is not to be underestimated. It is astonishingly ubiquitous and can be found at work in everything from the kind of mundane "what if" thinking we might engage in when deciding what to have for dinner, through to scientific reasoning (e.g. Einstein famously imagined himself chasing a light beam) or competing in the world "air guitar" championships (Guitar 2014). Carruthers (2011) has also argued that these forms of adult creative expression and childhood pretend play share common cognitive resources/origin, indeed, Vygotski (1978) argued that imagination is "internalised" pretend play. Further, this form of thinking may be a relatively recent evolutionary development which may have first appeared some 50 000 years ago and is responsible for the flowering of human creative thought which has continued ever since then.

This section seeks to make a case for the role of make-believe in the experience of presence. So, let us beginning by considering the experience of presence.

VR—virtual reality, or more fully the virtual reality triangle is defined by Burdea and Coiffet (2003), as comprising three components, namely, immersion, interaction and imagination.

Murray writes that immersion is a metaphorical term derived from the physical experience of being submerged in water. We seek the same feeling from a psychologically immersive experience that we do from a plunge in the ocean or swimming pool: the sensation of being surrounded by a completely other reality, as different as water is from air, that takes over all of our attention, our whole perceptual apparatus. (Murray 1997, p. 98).

Presence and Immersion

Early, formal definitions of telepresence, that is, the sense of presence created by technology have included, "the sense of 'being there'" (e.g. Held and Durlach 1992; Sheridan 1992); and famously as "the perceptual illusion of non-mediation" (Lombard and Ditton 1997) who wrote that, "An illusion of non-mediation occurs when a person fails to perceive or acknowledge the existence of a medium in his/her communication environment and responds as he/she would if the medium were not there". This description is highly reminiscent of both Norman (1999) *disappearing computer* design proposal and Heidegger's observation that when we are absorbed in activities such as hammering, the hammer and the nails disappear and only the hammering remains (Heidegger 1927/1962).

Presence has also been described as, "A mental state in which a user feels physically present within the computer-mediated environment" (Draper et al. 1998) and "the subjective experience of being in one place or environment, even when one is physically situated in another" (e.g. Witmer and Singer 1998). Further, and following Coleridge, Slater and Usoh (1994) have described presence as "the (suspension of dis-) belief" of being located in a world other than the physical one". As Riva (2009) notes, these accounts explicitly define presence as a consequence of using or interacting with the technology. This assumption, explicit or otherwise, also serves to define real world presence as the standard against which instances of this technologically-mediated presence (*mediated presence* hereafter) can be compared.

Theoretically rich accounts of presence

More recently, these early definitions have been challenged by more sophisticated and theoretically rich treatments. These are, of course, correspondingly much longer and more detailed than the initial, rather snappy, one-line definitions. For this reason, we will focus on only one of these and here the work of Riva and Waterworth is an obvious choice as it offers a particularly detailed and complex account. They began by posing the question, "What is the purpose of presence?" and have systematically answered it from a series of evolutionary-psychological, neuro-psychological and cognitive scientific perspectives. They argue that presence either evolved for no particular purpose (that is, as an emergent or serendipitous property of the nervous system) *or* it must offer evolutionary advantage. In examining the latter alternative, they note that *"the appearance of the sense of presence allows the nervous system to solve a key problem for its survival: how to differentiate between internal and external states"* (Riva et al. 2004).

From there they have drawn upon neuropsychology to propose a mapping between the different forms of self or "layers" of consciousness which Damaiso's work has uncovered and corresponding forms of presence (Damasio 1999). They have successively paired *proto*-presence, *core*-presence and *extended* presence onto the *proto*-self, *core*-self and *extended* self. With each step up this phylogenetic "ladder", the experience of presence becomes richer, more detailed and more recognisable. From here they recognise that the experience of presence is intuitive, that is, the product of unconscious and largely automatic cognitive processes. Thus, we do not make a conscious decision to be present in the world but find ourselves here as an immediate cognitive response. In recognising presence as an intuitive process, they also locate it within the dual-process accounts of cognition. These dual-process accounts comprise a broad family of theories which, while disagreeing in detail, do recognise that there are two basic forms of thinking, one is fast and intuitive (usually described as type or System 1 thinking) while the other is slow and deliberate (System 2 thinking). Most recently, they have added the dimension of embodiment into their account which seamlessly affords the integration of tools into the body schemata. The inclusion of Activity Theory also allows us to consider presence from the perspective of (human) objectives and goals (e.g. Riva 2009; Riva et al. 2004).

In all, Riva and his colleagues have a comprehensive and coherent account of real-world presence. Their work has located real world presence in a plausible evolutionary context and mapped expression of presence to different layers (self) of consciousness. This is a singular achievement. Other approaches have their own strengths and weaknesses but this work provides a flavour and overview of contemporary thinking in presence research. So far, we have only really considered real world presence, but what of the technologically mediated variety?

Make-believe and presence

Though we are usually present in the real world, we also frequently decide to immerse ourselves and to feel present in digital media. We argue that the means by which we feel present in these other "worlds" lies with our ability to imagine, to pretend and to make-believe. So, when we imagine we enter fictional worlds. These worlds may be not as vivid, immediate or as tangible as the real world, but they can be very engaging. These worlds are often solely the product of these abilities but very often they are directed and shaped by external media and artefacts such as toys, stories, other people and, of course, digital technology (Walton 1990).

These episodes of mediated presence are a consequence of cognitive decoupling and are "sandboxed"—or equivalent, in that they are labelled as imaginary. When we stop acting as-if we were there, we return to the real world. (*Before we develop this argument further, we should emphasize that we not are suggesting that pretending is in any sense concerned with deception or the wilful duping of innocent researchers*).

Let us consider the following two scenarios. The first of these is set in a children's tea party while the second considers the exploration of a virtual recreation of central London. In the first instance:

> A child proposes that she and her friends might hold a tea party. They agree to participate and equip themselves with toy tea cups and a toy teapot. The teapot is filled with water in lieu of tea. The children lay the tea set neatly on a tablecloth. One child acting as "mother" (the tea pourer) pours everyone a cup of "tea". As each child drinks from their a cup of "tea", they may then chat and perhaps share pretend "cake". As the "tea" is drunk, "mother" refills the empty cups. The party reaches its natural conclusion.

For the duration of the tea party the group of children have imagining that the water is tea, and they have behaved as if they were adults by imitating how they have seen their parents behave at a real tea party. Cups have been drunk from, emptied and refilled, conversations were enjoyed and "cake" may have been consumed. Having behaved as if they were at a tea-party, the children disperse.

In the second instance:

> A potential tourist using an immersive re-creation of London to get a sense of the city before booking a trip there. The tourist, in the immersive suite of the travel agent's premises, puts on a lightweight head-mounted display and a set of headphones and instantly finds themselves standing at the heart of Trafalgar Square. Looking around them they see pigeons completing a circuit around Nelson's Column before they head down Whitehall towards the river. The potential tourist is a little disappointed to find that it is not raining in London but is convinced enough that they want to go there in person.

For the duration of their trip to London, this tourist has imagined that he has engaged with a faithful representation of the city. They have imagined what they have seen and, within the constraints of the technology, they have acted as though they were there. While there are enormous differences between toy teacups and water in the first scenario and a head mounted display and a virtual model of London, there are also striking parallels too. In both instances the "players" decoupled the real world in favour of a fictional world. They act as they were engaged in a tea party and as though they were in Trafalgar Square. While imagination may not be the only psychological mechanism involved in mediated presence it is nonetheless central to its experience.

5.7 Conclusions

There can no doubt that the use of digital technologies requires us to engage them with our imaginations.

Prototyping may be the single most important and widely used technique in all of HCI. Prototyping enables us to progress from the sketchiest ideas to something which is all but complete. The early days of HCI had us drawing on paper, and mocking up with cardboard and this has developed into really very usable prototyping tools such as Axure® and Balsamiq® but at every turn these prototypes rely on our imagination to bring them to life. Using any prototype requires us to imagine them used in context (on the train or packed on a budget airliner) and used by real people (the young, the old or the barely literate) and for a purpose (booking or buying or sharing an image with someone).

Metaphor underpins the way in which we think and metaphor underpins the way in which user interfaces work. A metaphor enables us to use or say something in terms of something else and the only way we can communicate with digital technology is metaphorically and that requires us to use our imaginations. No imagination, no interaction.

There appears to be something wilful about HCI. It currently regards user experience (UX) as one of its most important aspects and includes terms like "anticipated" or "expected" experiences in its definition. Expectations and anticipations are the products of imagining ourselves in the near future (perhaps) using digital something other. Quite rightly these are part of the experience but mention of imagination is not. Surely these worlds of anticipation and expectation are the "imaginary worlds that can have a special relationship to reality—worlds in which we can extend, amplify, and enrich our own capacities to think, feel, and act" (Laurel 1993, p. 32).

Finally, as far as technology itself is concerned we have seen the advent of explicitly imaginary interfaces, but perhaps the most interesting case is that of virtual reality (VR). The experiences we have of VR are of other times, other places, with imaginary artefacts and imaginary representations and very occasionally with imaginary people. How we are able to do this requires more than powerful computers and high-resolution and precision peripherals. The missing element, however, is the contribution of our psychological faculties. Theories of immersion and presence have been developed which can account for the many of the findings from VR studies but I find it very difficult to (well, I just can't) understand why there is no mention of imagination which, after all, is the non-technological means of experiencing other times and other places.

References

Araujo B, Jota R, Perumal V, Yao JX, Singh K, Wigdor D (2016, February) Snake charmer: physically enabling virtual objects. In: Proceedings of the TEI'16: tenth international conference on tangible, embedded, and embodied interaction, pp. 218–226

Bach B, Sicat R, Beyer J, Cordeil M, Pfister H (2017) The hologram in my hand: how effective is interactive exploration of 3D visualizations in immersive tangible augmented reality? IEEE Trans Vis Comput Graph 24(1):457–467

Bekele MK, Champion E (2019) A comparison of immersive realities and interaction methods: cultural learning in virtual heritage. Front Robot AI 6:91

Binder T (1999) Setting the stage for improvised video scenarios, Ext. Abstracts CHI'99, 230–231

Boess S, Saakes D, Hummels C (2007) When is role playing really experiential?: case studies. In: Proceedings of the 1st international conference on Tangible and embedded interaction, February 2007. ACM, New York, pp 279–282

Buchenau M, Fulton Suri, J (2000) Experience prototyping. In: Proceedings of DIS 2000, pp 424–433

Burdea GC, Coiffet P (1994) Virtual reality technology. Wiley-Interscience, London

Burdea GC, Coiffet P (2003) Virtual reality technology. John Wiley & Son, New Jersey

Carroll JM, Mack RL (1985) Metaphor, computing systems, and active learning. Int J Man Mach Stud 22:39–57

Carruthers P (2011) Creative action in mind. Philos Psychol 24(4):437–461

Carter T, Seah SA, Long B, Drinkwater B, Subramanian S (2013) UltraHaptics: multi-point mid-air haptic feedback for touch surfaces. In: Proceedings of the 26th annual ACM symposium on User interface software and technology, October 2013. ACM, New York, pp 505–514

Damasio AR (1999) The feeling of what happens: body and emotion in the making of consciousness. Houghton Mifflin Harcourt

Dezfuli N, Khalilbeigi M, Huber J, Müller F, Mühlhäuser M (2012) PalmRC: imaginary palm-based remote control for eyes-free television interaction. In: Proceedings of the 10th European conference on interactive TV and video. ACM, New York, NY, USA, pp 27–34. https://doi.org/10.1145/2325616.2325623

Draper JV, Kaber DB, Usher JM (1998) Telepresence. Hum Factors 40(3):354–375

Ehn P (1988) Work oriented design of Computer Artifacts. Arbetslivscentrum, Stockholm

Fauconnier G, Turner M (2003) The way we think: conceptual blending and the mind's hidden complexities. Basic Books

Fishkin KP, Moran TP, Harrison BL (1998) Embodied user interfaces: Towards invisible user interfaces. In: IFIP international conference on engineering for human-computer interaction. Springer, Boston, MA, pp 1–18

Funk M, Kritzler M, Michahelles F (2017) HoloLens is more than air tap: Natural and intuitive interaction with holograms. In: Proceedings of the seventh international conference on the internet of things. ACM, p 31

Garry M, Manning CG, Loftus EF, Sherman SJ (1996) Imagination inflation: imagining a childhood event inflates confidence that it occurred. Psychon Bull Rev 3(2):208–214

Goff LM, Roediger HL (1998) Imagination inflation for action events: repeated imaginings lead to illusory recollections. Mem Cogn 26(1):20–33

Goffman E (1978) The presentation of self in everyday life. Harmondsworth, London

Guitar (2014) https://www.bbc.co.uk/newsround/28994245

Gustafson S, Bierwirth D, Baudisch P (2010) Imaginary interfaces: spatial interaction with empty hands and without visual feedback. In: Proceedings of the 23nd annual ACM symposium on user interface software and technology. ACM, New York

Gustafson S, Holz C, Baudisch P (2011) Imaginary phone: learning imaginary interfaces by transferring spatial memory from a familiar device. In: Proceedings of the 24th annual ACM symposium on user interface software and technology, October 2011. ACM, New York, pp 283–292

Gustafson SG, Rabe B, Baudisch PM (2013) Understanding palm-based imaginary interfaces: the role of visual and tactile cues when browsing. In: Proceedings of the SIGCHI conference on human factors in computing systems. ACM, New York, NY, USA, pp 889–898. https://doi.org/10.1145/2470654.2466114

Halasz F, Moran TP (1982) Analogy considered harmful. In: Proceedings of the 1982 conference on human factors in computing system. Gaithersburg, Maryland, United States, pp 383–386

Held RM, Durlach NI (1992) Telepresence. Presence: teleoperators and virtual environments 1(1):109–112

Heidegger M (1962) Being and time (Trans. John Macquarrie and Edward Robinson, 1927.). Harper, New York

Houde S, Hill C (1997) What do prototypes prototype?. In: Handbook of human-computer interaction. North-Holland, pp 367–381

Howard S, Carroll J, Murphy J, Peck J (2002) Using 'endowed props' in scenario-based design. In: Proceedings of the second Nordic conference on Human-computer interaction, October 2002. ACM, New York, pp 1–10

Joyce P (2003, June) Imagining experiences correctly. In: Proceedings of the Aristotelian society, vol 103, No. 1. Oxford University Press, Oxford, UK, pp 361–369

Kervegant C, Raymond F, Graeff D, Castet J (2017) Touch hologram in mid-air. In: ACM SIGGRAPH 2017 emerging technologies. ACM, p 23

Kim JR, Chan S, Huang X, Ng K, Fu LP, Zhao C (2019) Demonstration of refinity: an interactive holographic signage for new retail shopping experience. In: Extended abstracts of the 2019 CHI conference on human factors in computing systems. ACM, p INT007

Kuutti K, Iacucci G, Iacucci C (2002) Acting to know: improving creativity in the design of mobile services by using performances. In: Proceedings of creativity & cognition

Kumar SP, Pandithurai O (2013, February) Sixth sense technology. In 2013 international conference on information communication and embedded systems (ICICES), pp 947–953

Lakoff G, Johnson M (1980) Metaphors we live by. University of Chicago Press, Chicago

Laurel B (1993) Computers as theatre. Addison-Wesley Longman Publishing Co., Inc., Boston

Limerick H, Hayden R, Beattie D, Georgiou O, Müller J (2019) User engagement for mid-air haptic interactions with digital signage. In: Proceedings of the 8th ACM international symposium on pervasive displays. ACM, p 15

Lombard M, Ditton T (1997) At the heart of it all: the concept of presence. J Comput Med Commun 3(2):JCMC321

Lombard M, Ditton TB, Grabe ME, Reich RD (1997) The role of screen size in viewer responses to television fare. Commun Rep 10(1):95–106

Marcus A (1994) Metaphor mayhem: mismanaging, expectation and surprise. Interactions 41–43

Modell AH (2003) Imagination and the meaningful brain. MIT Press, Cambridge

Montano Murillo RA, Subramanian S, Martinez Plasencia D (2017, October) Erg-O: ergonomic optimization of immersive virtual environments. In: Proceedings of the 30th annual ACM symposium on user interface software and technology, pp. 759–771

Murray J (1997) Hamlet on the Holodeck, New York: The Free Press

Norman DA (1999) The invisible computer: why good products can fail, the personal computer is so complex, and information appliances are the solution. MIT press

Pedersen I, Gale N, Mirza-Babaei P, Reid S (2017) More than meets the eye: the benefits of augmented reality and holographic displays for digital cultural heritage. J Comput Cult Herit (JOCCH) 10(2):11

Popovici I, Schipor OA, Vatavu RD (2019) Hover: exploring cognitive maps and mid-air pointing for television control. Int J Hum Comput Stud 129:95–107

Rateau H, Grisoni L, De Araujo B (2014) Mimetic interaction spaces: controlling distant

Riva G (2009) Virtual reality: an experiential tool for clinical psychology. Br J Guidance Counselling 37(3):337–345

Riva G, Waterworth JA, Waterworth EL (2004) The layers of presence: a bio-cultural approach to understanding presence in natural and mediated environments. CyberPsychology Behav 7(4):402–416

Salvador T, Sato S (1999) Playacting and Focus Troupe: Theater techniques for creating quick, intense, immersive, and engaging focus group sessions. Interact ACM 6(5):35–41

Schipor OA, Vatavu RD (2018) Invisible, inaudible, and impalpable: users' preferences and memory performance for digital content in thin air. IEEE Pervasive Comput 17(4):76–85

Sheridan TB (1992) Musings on telepresence and virtual presence. Presence: Teleoperators Virtual Environ 1(1):120–126

Signer B, Curtin TJ (2017) Tangible holograms: towards mobile physical augmentation of virtual objects. arXiv preprint arXiv:1703.08288

Slater M, Usoh M (1994) Body centred interaction in immersive virtual environments. Artificial life and virtual reality, 1(1994):125–148

Slater M, Usoh M, Steed A (1994) Depth of presence in virtual environments. Presence: Teleoperators & Virtual Environ 3(2):130–144

Snyder C (2003) Paper prototyping: the fast and easy way to design and refine user interfaces. Morgan Kaufmann

Steins C, Gustafson S, Holz C, Baudisch P (2013) Imaginary devices: gesture-based interaction mimicking traditional input devices. In Proceedings of the 15th international conference on human-computer interaction with mobile devices and services, August 2013. ACM, New York, pp 123–126

Tognazzini B (1991) The art of human-computer interface design. Addison-Wesley, Reading

Vygotsky LS (1978) Mind in society: the development of higher psychological processes. Harvard University Press, Cambridge

Walton KL (1990) Mimesis as make-believe: on the foundations of the representational arts. Harvard University Press, Cambridge

Witmer BG, Singer MJ (1998) Measuring presence in virtual environments: a presence question-naire. Presence 7(3):225–240

Chapter 6
The Technological Imagination

Chapter Thumbnail

This final chapter is concerned with two kinds of "what-if" questions.

The first of these focus on the speculative questions which have realisable answers, so an example would be: what if we could interact with our TV (or any other home technology) by simply speaking to it or gesturing at it? These first kinds of questions have received our attention in Chaps. 3, 3 and 5. Some are at the speculative end of HCI, but others are pretty much mainstream. Although these technologies rely on imagination and make-believe, the literature, of course, offers little or no mention of their contribution in the operation of the associated technologies.

The second kinds of speculative questions reject the very idea of technological solutions and these are the *design fictions*. Design fictions have numerous but more-or-less complementary definitions: for some they are design research tools; for others they are intended to be provocative prototypes which bridge the modern world and the make-believe world described in science fiction; for others, they are "never to be commercial" thought experiments. All-in-all, they are speculative, that is, they are products of our imaginations. Indeed, more than anywhere else in HCI, we find frequent reference to the imaginary and the fictional. They occupy the extreme end of the technological imagination which I cannot help but imagine is the left side, the sinister end of the spectrum.

6.1 Introduction

Imagination may have arisen on the savannas of Africa to enable our ancestors to plan the next day's hunt, or make sense of the behaviour of our group and as such it will have offered a very simple and direct survival advantage—it enabled us to cope. But how does this translate into our burgeoning post-industrial, technological society? The simple answer is that in many ways it is unchanged, and recalling Vygotsky's

© Springer Nature Switzerland AG 2020

P. Turner, *Imagination + Technology*, Human–Computer Interaction Series, https://doi.org/10.1007/978-3-030-37348-1_6

observation that everything in the artefactual world is a product of imagination, it continues to cope very well.

The discussion in this chapter on the nature of the technological imagination is in 2 parts.

6.2   Part I: Imagining the Possible

Imagination necessarily (indeed, must) underpins the conception, envisagement, prototyping, design, creation, evaluation, critique, dissemination, appropriation, repair and re-use and ultimately the decommissioning and recycling of digital technology. This may be the one factor which is common to every phase of its lifecycle. Well-designed or not, interesting or dull, essential or trivial, digital products are the products of our imagination. But more than this, we rely on our imaginations to use and experience it too. We cannot just pick up and use a digital artefact without the imaginative expectation of what will happen when we, say, press < the green power button > or swipe a screen. This expectation, along with the anticipation of what might go wrong, is what Adamski and Westrum (2003) call the "requisite imagination". What's more digital technology is different from other kinds of technology in we do not and cannot use it directly. While we can easily pick up a hammer, or knife and fork and use them, we cannot necessarily do the same with a smart phone (except, perhaps to use it as a door stop or as a projectile). We use phones and all other digital technology by way of an interface which in turn relies on an interaction metaphor (or more usually, a series of metaphors), for example, "this technology is like a so-and-so" … or "cut the image from here and paste it there …" (and this is in the absence of a sharp-edged tool and a paste-pot). Both examples suggest a degree of indirection ("like a") and a repertoire of actions which only resemble real-world behaviour (we act as-if or we pretend as though we do so for real).

Other people

Laurel writes, "Thinking about interfaces is thinking too small. Designing human-computer experience isn't about building a better desktop. It's about creating imaginary worlds that have a special relationship to reality–worlds in which we can extend, amplify, and enrich our own capacities to think, feel, and act." This quotation is from Laurel's *Computers as Theatre* (1993), where she continues, "Theatre is about interaction, about themes and conflicts, goals and approaches to those goals, frustration, success, tension, and then the resolution of those tensions. Theatre is dynamic, changing, always in motion. Our modern technologies with their powerful computers, multiple sensors, communication links and displays are also about interaction, and treating that interaction as theatre proves to be rich, enlightening and powerful." We cannot help but agree with these sentiments, primarily because at bottom, they are based on our ability to imagine and make-believe.

We also note that we share the products of our imaginations with each other. Indeed, it is difficult to imagine having a bright idea without being able to share it (or at the very least to lease it) with someone else. This is primarily mediated by way of stories which themselves are supported by props including pictures, dance, ritual, artefacts, music and so forth. This kind of shared imagination has been further energised in recent years with the appearance of digital media which Rose (2011) has observed, "is the first medium that can be all media. It can be text, or audio, or video, or all of the above".

Augmentation

Finally, artefacts of all kinds can augment and even supplant our imaginations. Perhaps the earliest examples of cave art or carefully incised and traced animal bones, or the stained-glass windows of medieval churches in Europe. It is easy to imagine our ancestors using these props in retelling the story of an eventful hunting expedition; or the Warka vase being used to plan a religious procession; or priests telling Bible stories about the promise of post-mortem paradise. These images and artefacts serve to reinforce the imagination of those gazing upon them, just as the current generation of digital technologies with its variations of reality (augmented, virtual or mixed) offering themselves as an even more powerful ways of bringing to life our patchy, incomplete and all too often, sad little imaginations.

Care

We have also noted that our imagination is concernful. We shift or adopt perspectives with other people not out of idle curiosity but because we are involved. We are, for example, concerned about the outcome (for us), so perspective shifting is more appropriate for this discussion. To be concernful is to recognise the interconnectedness of activities and use of tools in the broader context of other people, other technologies and other contexts. This, of course, is the substance of "involvement" and this involvement with technology enables us to encounter it as available or ready-to-hand. To be ready-to-hand means that we encounter/ experience technology as being proximal or handy and as being available for immediate use or action. More specifically, the degree of involvement, however, does vary depending upon how engaging (and available) the digital technology is. Indeed, this entire description of involvement-engagement hinges on the nature of this availability. For Heidegger, all human activity is located in a "web of significance", or "context of equipment" comprising inter-related items of technology which are perceived as being useful in order to complete tasks. From this reading, involvement with technology is an inevitable, unavoidable consequence being alive and well, in the world. Thus, most of us have not adopted a theoretical stance with respect to technology because we are (already) involved with it. However, consistent with just about all forms of new and emerging digital technology, mention of imagination is absent, so we are again reminded of the reluctance so many disciplines have for engaging with imagination. So, perhaps we have articulated something we have long known or at least half suspected: imagination is important but unless we are engaged in something creative or explicitly concerned with problem solving, we largely ignore it. HCI certainly has.

This brings us to the second half of our argument.

6.3   Part II: Imagining the Improbable (Design Fictions)

The second half of the technological imagination (and this argument) consists of those ideas which are not intended to answer research questions as such but are designed to provoke or rephrase them or even ask fresh ones. These are the design fictions. As design fictions are still evolving, and there are no firm definitions, we will take this opportunity to contribute a few thoughts of our own as to their use and constitution.

Reference to design fictions appears in both HCI and interaction design, where there is discussion and there is no little confusion around the idea (e.g. Bleecker 2009; Blythe 2014) and reflects what Hales describes as a "speculative turn" though it is also called the "cultural turn". Hales (2013), introducing a special issue of the journal Digital Creativity on design fiction, writes that it is enticing, provocative and elusive and that "it creates a discursive space within which new forms of cultural artefact (futures) might emerge".

However, design fictions are not used to explore future (imaginary) prototypes as potential solutions to emerging problems, instead (and this is not without controversy) they are used as a research tool to ask better, more searching questions. They may include, but are not limited to, texts, movies, prototypes of varying degrees of realisation, above all, they are not in themselves intended to become finished products, but rather as provocations to conversation about the technical future. (A first taxonomy of design fictions may be found in Hales 2013.)

Sterling (2009) defined design fiction as the "deliberate use of diegetic prototypes to suspend disbelief about change" (that Coleridge quotation again). Key to making sense of this is appreciating that *diegesis* simply refers to the storyworld created as a background narrative or context or more simply, plot. Thus, a diegetic prototype is a prototype that exists within the storyworld and, "suspending disbelief" about change, is congruent with speculative design. Thus, the role of design fiction is "not to show how things will be but to open up a space for discussion". The suspension of disbelief jars as we might expect those who are employing design fictions to be enthusiastic about make-belief and would not be bother by pangs of "disbelief". Anyway, let's begin with an example illustrated in the image below. The "rock and rollover" design fiction is from a project reported in Blythe et al. (2015), where researchers worked with older people in exploring digital support for positive ageing. The fiction here takes the form of "advertisements for products and services that do not exist", one of which (a care home) its shown in Fig. 6.1.

Early elaboration

Bleecker (2009) was the first to write a comprehensive essay on design fiction which was to quickly become fairly influential. In his, "A short essay on design, science, fact and fiction" he writes "Design fiction is a way of exploring different approaches to making things, probing the material conclusions of your imagination, removing the usual constraints when designing for massive market commercialization—the ones that people in blue shirts and yellow ties call "realistic." This is a different genre of design. Not realism, but a genre that is forward looking, beyond incremental

Fig. 6.1 Design fictions for ageing well: the KISS care home advertisement, image by kind permission Jamie Steane and Mark Blythe

and makes an effort to explore new kinds of social interaction rituals. As much as science fact tells you what is and is not possible, design fiction understands constraints differently. Design fiction is about creative provocation, raising questions, innovation, and exploration". For Bleecker, the conversation around design futures should be rooted in the social and the cultural, rather corralled by the technological. He argues that for this to happen, the creators of design fictions should learn from science fiction, both in terms of engaging narrative and creative invention. Here we introduce Kirby's (2010) take on a *diegetic prototype* which is defined as a prototype that "demonstrates to large public audiences a technology's need, benevolence and viability". Such prototypes depict technologies which are real and functional within the context of the story.

Bleecker offers a number of examples of design fictions which may help here, including the Near Future Laboratory's "Slow Messenger", which is an exploration of the experience of hand-held messaging. Here, messages are received character by character, over a period that ranges from seconds to days per character, the pace of being inversely related to the emotional content of the message. Bleecker comments that while such a device may be thought preposterous, it provokes "conversations and considerations about the sometimes-overwhelming communications practices of mobile and instant messaging." A more recent example of fictional technology is "Blind Camera" by the designer Sascha Pohflepp. The camera cannot take photographs itself, since it has no lens but captures and presents on its screen other people's photographs that were taken at the moment that the Blind Camera's button was pressed. The fiction was designed to prompt speculation upon the meaning of photographs and the associated interaction rituals.

In their 10 year review of design fictions, Lindley and Coulton (2015) tell us that although they are still poorly defined, a design fiction:

1. Is something that creates a story world;
2. has something being prototyped within that story world;
3. does so in order to create a discursive space.

Although this definition appears straightforward, complexity arrives when we consider what 'something' may be—and we believe it is this complexity that is circumvented in discourses that characterise design fiction as 'up for grabs' or 'open to different interpretations'.

While story worlds may be created in a variety of ways, design fiction has undoubtedly been heavily influenced by Hollywood's diegetic prototypes, but this should not be understood as being limited to film-based prototypes. Markussen and Knutz (2014) describe using a variety of media including text, video, objects and graphics, as 'packaging' for design fiction stories. Additionally, abstracts and conclusions to academic papers have been used as the substrate for design fictions exploring the possible unintended consequences of HCI research. Meanwhile other examples build assemblages to craft the story world in multiple media simultaneously.

Blythe (2014) suggested in his *Research Through Design Fiction* that fictional studies of prototypes might serve as a useful alternative to actually building them. His paper described "imaginary abstracts" that were effectively pastiches of contemporary Research Through Design projects.

Non-textual design fictions

Reading the Atlantic magazine some 70 years ago, one would have come across a prototype memory augmentation system. Bush (1945) conducted a "thought experiment" (which shares many of the attributes of design fictions) with a mashup of the available technology of the day to create the 'memex' system. Memex looks like a cross between an antique personal computer and a radiogram.[1] Let us consider an extended quotation from this famous paper for a moment. *"Consider a future device for individual use, which is a sort of mechanized private file and library. It needs a name, and, to coin one at random, "memex" will do. A memex is a device in which an individual stores all his books, records, and communications, and which is mechanized so that it may be consulted with exceeding speed and flexibility. It is an enlarged intimate supplement to his memory. It consists of a desk, and while it can presumably be operated from a distance, it is primarily the piece of furniture at which he works. On the top are slanting translucent screens, on which material can be projected for convenient reading. There is a keyboard, and sets of buttons and levers. Otherwise it looks like an ordinary desk. In one end is the stored material. The matter of bulk is well taken care of by improved microfilm. Only a small part of the interior of the memex is devoted to storage, the rest to mechanism. Yet if the user inserted 5000 pages of material a day it would take him hundreds of years to fill the repository, so he can be profligate and enter material freely."*

This description of the memex presents an interesting vision of the augmentation of human memory. Memex is where "all his books, records, and communications" are kept on "improved microfilm" with a project storage capacity of less than 400 Gb. In essence memex was the first vision of an electronic memory prosthetic. Realisations of different aspects of this concept are readily available. For example, Microsoft's SenseCam technology which lies at the heart of their MyLifeBits programme Bell

---

[1] Wikipedia claims that a radiogram is known as a *console* in the US (https://en.wikipedia.org/wiki/Radiogram_(device)).

and Gemmell (2007) is a device that captures up to 2000 images per day together with contextual data. MyLifeBits can, in principle, store a lifetime's worth of anything that can be digitised. Advances in storage technology have removed the barrier to collecting 'everything', as a Microsoft Research spokesperson has recently observed "you can store every conversation you've ever had in a terabyte. You can store every picture you've ever taken in another terabyte. And the net present value of a terabyte is $200." So, a lifetime's worth of data may be stored for as little as $400 (FutureWire 2005). So, fifteen years later we are now confident that the extended memory features that this technology offers were to become ubiquitous (not sure where—look at your phone).

The other example of non-textual design fictions is "Tomorrow's World" which was a weekly TV programme broadcast by the BBC which ran from the mid-1960s for almost forty years. It offered "visions of the future" and technology reviews and demonstrations for a general audience and its tone was set by one of its first presenters who was a former wartime Spitfire pilot. I have a clear memory of being promised that virtual reality technology would be widespread in the near future and that *it would change everything*. Had they been available, Tomorrow's World might well have included the sort of developments now described (e.g. imaginary interfaces) in the preceding section, but much of the programmes content could be described as optimistic *design fictions*.

Consumer research

Wong and Mulligan (2016) have reported on the use of concept videos as a form of design fiction. In 2012, Google announced Google Glass which was an augmented reality set of spectacles and the announcement took the form of a concept video published on YouTube. The video showed what a wearer of this AR headset might experience. This qualifies as a design fiction because at the time of the video, Google Glass did not exist.

Indeed, Google did not make Glass available to the public until 2014. Similarly, a concept video on YouTube was used by Microsoft to announce their augmented reality headset, HoloLens (their AR system). Glass and HoloLens share a number of features but Glass was portrayed as an everyday tool, while HoloLens was presented as more oriented towards gaming or work. Wong and Mulligan argue that the concept videos acted like design fictions.

6.4   Final Words and Future Work

Throughout this book we have adopted a single person perspective on imagination which reflects the nature of the reported work. While we did make occasional reference to imagination being mediated or crystallised by way of psychological and material props and it being distributed across external representations, our account of imagination reflects the individual alone. Yet, while there can be little doubt that imagination is (for example) an embodied cognitive facility, the basic research into this intuition is, as we have come to expect, absent. Instead, there is mention of make-believe but only as the "behavioural aspect of imagination". This is woefully inadequate.

Further work on gesture

We should establish an appropriate conceptual framework for imagination, locating it in a contemporary cognitive scientific thinking. Though we can only but speculate what such an account might look like, it should be able to find a place for, say, the role of gesture in imagination. We have chosen to explore gesture because it combines aspects of the cognitive, the embodied, the external, the enactive and the playful, all of which traditional cognitive or social psychology might struggle to accommodate.

We begin with the work of Goldin-Meadow (2005, pp. 136–149) who introduces gesture by noting that we do so talking on the phone (when the other person cannot see us); we gesture when we talk to ourselves; we gesture in the dark and people who have been blind from birth spontaneously gesture. So, she concludes, to treat gesture as a simple adjunct to communication does not do it justice. Rauscher et al. (1996) found, unsurprisingly, that when people are prevented from gesturing when describing a spatial scene, they showed significantly poorer fluency in their descriptions than those who were able to gesture freely. Similarly, Goldin-Meadow and her colleagues (2011) reported an experiment in which they have contrasted the abilities of two matched groups of children to memorise a list and then carry out some mathematical problem solving before recalling the list. The children were assigned to either free-to-gesture and no-gesture condition. The free-to-gesture group recalled noticeably more in the memory test. Furthermore, they tell us that there is evidence which indicates that the level of gesturing increases with task difficulty; and that gesturing is seen to increase when speakers must choose between options; and that gesturing increases when reasoning about a problem rather than merely describing the problem or known solution. Goldin-Meadow accounts for these data by suggesting that gesturing reduces the cognitive load by scaffolding our cognition. She writes, "gesture … expands the set of representational tools available to speakers and listeners. It can redundantly reflect information represented through verbal formats or it can augment that information, adding nuances possible though visual and motor formats" (2003, p. 186), and this must be true of imagining too.

Hostetter and Alibali (2008) have suggested that gesture is simulated action (or as we prefer, pretending) and have distinguished among three forms of gesture which they claim underpins language and mental imagery. They divide gesture into three categories namely: representational gestures—that is, movements that represent the content of speech by pointing to a referent in the physical environment (deictic gestures), depicting a referent with the motion or shape of the hands (iconic gestures), or depicting a concrete referent or indicating a spatial location for an abstract idea (metaphoric gestures); and beat gestures (movements that emphasize the prosody or structure of speech without conveying semantic information); and interactive gestures (that is, movements used to manage turn taking and other aspects of an interaction between multiple speakers). In essence, gesture reflects what is possible, given that familiar mix of our bodies and the physical environment.

Charades
A for the intimacy of imagination and gesture, here we can consider the work of De Jaegher and Di Paolo (2007) on the game of charades. This game involves a pantomime with players having to "act out" a phrase without speaking, while the other members of the same team try to guess what the phrase is. So, let us suppose that the phrase is the title of a film with two words. The player would then be expected to use the standard gesture for a movie by emulating the operation of an old-style projector (that is, imitating the shape of a lens with one hand and performing a winding motion with the other). Once the word "movie" had been spoken, the player would indicate the number two by tapping his or her arm with two fingers). And on the game would run. These gestures are readily and easily interpreted.

Metaphor
Here, Modell picks up the argument. He proposes that "the metaphoric process that we recognize in our dreams continuously operates while we are awake". If we assume that our experiences are stored as unconscious autobiographical memories then he proposes that they are only reached by means of metaphor. He goes on to define metaphor as central to the operation of imagination. Metaphor, he tells us, is "a mapping or transfer of meaning between dissimilar domains (from a source domain to a target domain)". This much is pretty much standard and agrees with the current thinking on the nature of metaphor but he continues, "Metaphor not only transfers meaning between different domains, but by means of novel re-combinations metaphor can transform meaning and generate new perceptions. Imagination could not exist without this re-combinatory metaphoric process". He sees imagination as being an unconscious neural process and that the metaphors which it employs are generated from the body's experiences (he uses the word "feelings").

Collective imagining
Finally, work reported by Nemirovsky et al. (2012) argues for the role of gesture in what they term *collective* imagining, by which the subjects of imagination are not just simulated as Hostetter and Alibali propose, but co-created, co-constructed and brought into quasi-presence for the participants. Gestures are constitutive of *phantasms*, which are viewed as imaginary, quasi-present entities, distributed across media and modalities and shared among participants. For these authors, "*imagining is (a) a purposeful and socio-materially mediated process, (b) distributed across multiple, mutually elaborating elements [...] (c) can be collaborative [...], and (d) is intimately rooted in possibilities for perceptuomotor engagement with both real and imagined objects or events.*" Their conclusions are supported by empirical evidence from a study of shared interaction with an interactive drawing tool.

Towards a credible account
As we have already seen, Johnson (2013) argues that imagination is an important, indeed necessary, component of "an adequate account of meaning and rationality" and its absence is a significant obstacle. He has proposed the following components are needed in any adequate account of imagination. These are (preserving his order): (i) Categorisation. This is the recognition that we tend to break up our experiences

into kinds; (ii) Schemata (knowledge structures); (iii) Metaphoric projection. We use metaphor to create connections (which he describes as "projection") across schemata; (iv) Metonymy and (v) Narrative structure. As a list this is difficult to argue with but any credible, comprehensive model should be able to account not only for the components of Johnson's list, but should also recognise that imagination is a full-blown 4E (embodied, enactive, embedded and external) form of cognition and only by beginning there can we hope to describe the complex, reciprocal and dynamic relationship between digital technology and imagination.

References

Adamski A, Westrum R (2003) Requisite imagination. The fine art of anticipating what might go wrong. In: Handbook of cognitive task design, pp 193–220

Bell G, Gemmell J (2007) A digital life. Scien American, 296(3):58–65

Bleecker J (2009) Design fiction: a short essay on design, science, fact and fiction. Near Future Lab 29

Blythe MA (2014) Research through design fiction: narrative in real and imaginary abstracts. In: Proceedings of the SIGCHI conference on human factors in computing systems. ACM, pp 703–712

Blythe M, Steane J, Roe J, Oliver C (2015, April) Solutionism, the game: design fictions for positive aging. In: Proceedings of the 33rd annual ACM conference on human factors in computing systems, pp 3849–3858

Bush V (1945) As we may think. Atl Mon 176(1):101–108

De Jaegher H, Di Paolo E (2007) Participatory sense-making. Phenomenol Cogn Sci 6(4):485–507

Futurewire (2005). futurewire.blogspot.com/2005/04/your-life-in-bits.html. Accessed 25 Sept 2019

Goldin-Meadow S (2005) Hearing gesture: how our hands help us think. Harvard University Press, Cambridge

Goldin-Meadow S (2011) Learning through gesture. Wiley Interdiscip Rev Cogn Sci 2(6):595–607

Hales D (2013) Design fictions an introduction and provisional taxonomy. Digital Creativity 24(1):1–10

Hostetter AB, Alibali MW (2008) Visible embodiment: gestures as simulated action. Psychon Bull Rev 15(3):495–514

Johnson M (2013) The body in the mind: the bodily basis of meaning, imagination, and reason. University of Chicago Press

Kirby D (2010) The future is now: diegetic prototypes and the role of popular films in generating real-world technological development. Soc Stud Sci 40(1):41–70

Knutz E, Markussen T (2014) The role of fiction in experiments within design, art & architecture-towards a new typology of design fiction. Artifact: J Des Pract 3(2):8–1

Laurel B (1993) Computers as theatre. Addison-Wesley Longman Publishing Co., Inc., Boston, MA

Lindley J, Coulton P (2015) Back to the future: 10 years of design fiction. In: Proceedings of the 2015 British HCI conference. ACM, pp 210–211

Nemirovsky R, Kelton ML, Rhodehamel B (2012) Gesture and imagination: on the constitution and uses of phantasms. Gesture 12(2):130–165

Rauscher FH, Krauss RM, Chen Y (1996) Gesture, speech, and lexical access: the role of lexical movements in speech production. Psychol Sci 70:226–231

Rose P (2011) Digital (A) literacy. E-Learn Digital Media 8(3):258–270

Sterling B (2009) Design fiction. Interactions 16(3):20–24

Wong RY, Mulligan DK (2016) When a product is still fictional: anticipating and speculating futures through concept videos. In: Proceedings of the 2016 ACM conference on designing interactive systems. ACM, pp 121–133

Further Readings

Beardsley MC (1969) Aesthetic experience regained. J Aesthet Art Crit 28:3–11

Berntsen D, Bohn A (2010) Remembering and forecasting: the relation between autobiographical memory and episodic future thinking. Mem Cogn 38:265–278

Binder T, Setting the stage for improvised video scenarios. In: Ext. Abstracts CHI'99, pp 230–231

Bluck S, Alea N, Habermas T, Rubin DC (2005) A tale of three functions: the self–reported uses of autobiographical memory. Soc Cogn 23(1):91–117

Blythe MA, Wright PC (2006) Pastiche scenarios: Fiction as a resource for user centered design. Interact Comput 18:1139–1164

Bødker S, Christiansen E (1997) Scenarios as springboards in CSCW design. In: Bowker G, Star SL, Turner W, Gasser L (eds) Social science, technical systems, and cooperative work: beyond the great divide, LEA, pp 217–234

Boletsis C, Karahasanovic A, Fjuk A (2017) Virtual bodystorming: utilizing virtual reality for prototyping in service design. In: International conference on augmented reality, virtual reality and computer graphicsm, June 2017. Springer, Cham, pp 279–288

Brandt E, Grunnet C, Evoking the future: drama and props in user centered design. In: Proceedings of participatory design conference (PDC'00), pp 11–20

Brewley WL, Roberts TL, Schroit D, Verplank W (1983) Human factors testing in the design of xerox's 8010 'star' office workstation. In: Proceedings of the Chi'83 conference

Brooks P (1992) Reading for the plot: design and intention in narrative. Harvard University Press

Burns C, Dishman E, Verplank W, Lassiter B (1994). Actors, hairdos & videotape—informance design. In: Conference companion on Human factors in computing systems, Apr 1994. ACM, pp 119–120

Button G (ed) (1992) Technology and working order: studies of work, interaction and technology. Routledge, London

Card SK, Moran TP, Newell A (1983) The psychology of human-computer interaction. Hillsdale, LEA, New Jersey

Carroll JM (2000) Making use: scenario-based design of human-computer interaction. IEEE Computer Society Press, Los Alamitos, CA

Carruthers, Smith P (eds) Theories of theories of mind. Cambridge University Press

Chen IB (1984) Florence nightingale. Sci Am 250(3):128–37. https://www.scientificamerican.com/magazine/sa/1984/03-01/

Chu SL, Quek F (2013) Things to imagine with: designing for the child's creativity. In: Proceedings of the 12th international conference on interaction design and children, June 2013. ACM, pp 261–264

Clemmensen T (2004) Four approaches to user modelling—a qualitative research interview study of HCI professionals' practice. Interact Comput 16:799–829

Cosmides L, Tooby J (2000) Consider the source: the evolution of adaptations for decoupling and metarepresentation. In: Sperber D (ed) Metarepresentations: a multidisciplinary Perspective. Oxford University Press, Oxford, UK

Daniels H (2017) Preview. More editions

D'Argembeau A, Van der Linden M (2004) Phenomenal characteristics associated with projecting oneself back into the past and forward into the future: influence of valence and temporal distance

Decety J, Jeannerod J, Prablanc C (1989) The timing of mentally represented actions. Behav Brain Res 34:35–42

Djajadiningrat JP, Gaver WW, Fres JW (2000) Interaction relabelling and extreme characters: methods for exploring aesthetic interactions. In: Proceedings of the conference on designing interactive systems: processes, practices, methods, and techniques, 17–19 Aug 2000. New York City, New York, United States, pp 66–71

Dreyfuss H (1955) Designing for people. Erni Peter, New York

Egan A (2008) Imagination, delusion, and self-deception. In: Bayne, Fernandez (eds) Delusion and self-deception: affective influences on belief-formation. Psychology Press, pp 263–280

Esses VM, Haddock G, Zanna MP (1993) Values, stereotypes, and emotions as determinants of intergroup attitudes. In: Mackie DM, Hamilton DL (eds) Affect, cognition, and stereotyping: interactive processes in group perception. Academic Press, San Diego, CA, pp 137–166

Fine GA (2002) Shared fantasy: role playing games as social worlds. University of Chicago Press

Finke RA (1996) Imagery, creativity, and emergent structure. Conscious Cogn 5(3):381–393

Floyd IR, Jones MC, Twidale MB (2004) Resolving incommensurable debates: a preliminary identification of persona kinds. Attrib Charact Artifact 2(1):12–26

Friedman B, Hendry D (2012) The envisioning cards: a toolkit for catalyzing humanistic and technical imaginations. In: Proceedings of the SIGCHI conference on human factors in computing systems. ACM, pp 1145–1148

Garcia-Marques LA, Santos SC, Mackie D (2006) Stereotypes: static abstractions or dynamic knowledge structures. J Pers Soc Psychol 91:814–831

Gatzia DE, Sotnak E (2014) Fictional truth and make-believe. Philosophia 42(2):349–361

Gentner D, Markman AB (1997) Structure mapping in analogy and similarity. Am Psychol 52(1):45–56

Giora R, Fein O, Kronrod A, Elnatan I, Shuval N, Zur A (2004) Weapons of mass distraction: optimal innovation and pleasure ratings. Metaphor Symb 19(2):115–141

Goel V (1995) Sketches of thought. MIT Press, Cambridge, MA

Gombrich EHJ (1963) Meditations on a hobby horse and other essays on the theory of art. Phaidon, London

Govers PC, Mugge R (2004) I love my Jeep, because its tough like me: The effect of product-personality congruence on product attachment. In: Proceedings of the fourth international conference on design and emotion. Ankara, Turkey, pp 12–14

Grosjean S, Fixmer P, Brassac C (2000) Those psychological tools inside the design process. Knowl-Based Syst 13:3–9. Elsevier Science

Gruberger M, Simon EB, Levkovitz Y, Zangen A, Hendler T (2011) Towards a neuroscience of mind-wandering. Front Hum Neurosci 5:56

Grudin J, Pruitt J (2002) Personas, participatory design and product development: an infrastructure for engagement. In: Proceedings of PDC, vol 2, June 2002

Hallnäs L (2011) On the foundations of interaction design aesthetics: Revisiting the notions of form and expression. Int J Des 5(1):73–84

Hamilton DL, Sherman JW (1994) Stereotypes. In: Wyer JRS, Srull TK (eds) Handbook of social cognition, 2nd edn. Macmillan, Hillsdale, NJ, pp 1–68

Harpur P (2002) The philosophers' secret fire. The Squeeze Press, Glastonbury, Somerset

Hartmann J, Sutcliffe A, de Angeli A (2008) Towards a theory of user judgment of aesthetics and user interface quality. ACM Trans Computer–Human Interact 15(4) (Article No. 15)

Hekkert P, Snelders D, Van Wieringen PCW (2003) 'Most advanced, yet acceptable': Typicality and novelty as joint predictors of aesthetic preference in industrial design. Br J Psychol 94:111–124

Herman D (2009) Basic elements of narrative. Wiley-Blackwell, Oxford

Higham T, Basell L, Jacobi R, Wood R, Ramsey CB, Conard NG (2012) Testing models for the beginnings of the Aurignacian and the advent of figurative art and music: the radiocarbon chronology of Geißenklösterle. J Hum Evol 62(6):664–676

Hobbes T (2006) Leviathan. A&C Black

Hoffman HG, Patterson DR, Seibel E, Soltani M, Jewett-Leahy L, Sharar SR (2008) Virtual reality pain control during burn wound debridement in the hydrotank. Clin J Pain 24(4):299–304

Holt DB, Schor J (2000) The consumer society reader. New Press, New York

Hume D (1740/2009). A treatise of human nature: being an attempt to introduce the experimental method of reasoning into moral subjects. The Floating Press

Hynes CA, Baird AA, Grafton ST (2006) Differential role of the orbital frontal lobe in emotional versus cognitive perspective-taking. Neuropsychologia 44(3):374–383

IEEE Pervasive Computing (17(4), Oct–Dec 1 2018: 76–85 Oct–Dec 1 2018)

ISO (1999) ISO 13407: Human-centred design processes for interactive systems. Geneva: International Standards Organisation. Available from the British Standards Institute, London

ISO 9241-210 (2010)

Jeannerod M (2006) Motor cognition: what actions tell to the self. Oxford University Press, Oxford

Johnson J, Roberts TL, Verplank W, Irby CH, Beard M, Mackey K (1989) The xerox star: a retrospective. IEEE Comput

Johnson MK, Foley MA, Suengas AG, Raye CL (1988) Phenomenal characteristics of memories for perceived and imagined autobiographical events. J Exp Psychol Gen 117(4):371

Kaiser HF (1960) The application of electronic computers to factor analysis. Educ Psychol Measur 20(2):141–151

Karwowski M, Soszynski M (2008) How to develop creative imagination? assumptions, aims and effectiveness of role play training in creativity (RPTC). Think Ski Creat 3(2):163–171

Kavakli M, Scrivener S et al (1998) Structure in idea sketching behavior. Des Stud 19(4):485–517

Kay A (1995) The problems with metaphor Interactions 5(1):56

Kensing F, Blomberg J (1998) Participatory design: issues and concerns. Comput Support Coop Work (CSCW 7(3–4):167–185

Klinger E (1971) Structure and functions of fantasy. Wiley, New York

Kosslyn SM, Ganis G, Thompson WL (2001) Neural foundations of imagery. Natl Rev Neurosci 2:635–642

Kosslyn SM (1980) Image and mind. Harvard University Press

Kosslyn SM, Ball TM, Reiser BJ (1978) Visual images preserve metric spatial information: evidence from studies of image scanning. J Exp Psychol Hum Percept Perform 4:47–60

Kozlowski LT, Bryant KJ (1977) Sense of direction, spatial orientation, and cognitive maps. J Exp Psychol: Hum Percept Perform 3(4):590–598

Kung P (2010) Imagining as a guide to possibility. Research 81(3):620–663

Langdon P, Lewis T, Clarkson PJ (2007) The effects of prior experience on the use of consumer products. Univ Access Inf Soc 6(2):179–191

Langland-Hassan P (2012) Pretense, imagination, and belief: the single attitude theory. Philos Stud 159(2):155–179

Lee S, Koubek RJ (2010) Understanding user preferences based on usability and aesthetics before and after actual use. Interact Comput 22:530–543

Lessiter J, Freeman J, Keogh E, Davidoff J (2001) A cross-media presence questionnaire: the ITC-sense of presence inventory. Presence: Teleoperators Virtual Environ 10(3):282–297

Liang C-C, Chang CM, Chang Y, Lin L-J (2012) The exploration of imagination indicators. Turk Online J Educ Technol 11(3):366–374

Liao SY, Gendler TS (2011) Pretense and imagination. Wiley Interdiscip Rev: Cogn Sci 2(1):79–94

Lieberman JN (1977/2014) Playfulness: its relationship to imagination and creativity. Educational psychology series. Academic Press, New York

Malle BF (2004) How the mind explains behaviour. MIT Press, Cambridge, USA

Mariano-Mello Tarcilla, Ramírez-Correa Patricio, Rondan-Cataluña Francisco (2018) Effect of aesthetics on the purchase intention of smartphones. Informacion Tecnologica 29:227–236

Matthews B (2007) Locating design phenomena: a methodological excursion. Des Stud 28:369–385

McAlpine H, Cash P, Hicks B (2017) The role of logbooks as mediators of engineering design work. Des Stud 48:1–29. https://doi.org/10.1016/j.destud.2016.10.003

McGown A, Green G et al (1998) Visible Ideas: information patterns of conceptual sketch activity. Des Stud 19(4):431–453

McQuaid HL, Aradhana G, McManus M (2003) When you can't talk to customers: using storyboards and narratives to elicit empathy for users. In: Proceedings of the 2003 international conference on designing pleasurable products and interfaces, pp 120–125

Michaelian K (2016) Mental time travel: episodic memory and our knowledge of the personal past. MIT Press

Mithen SJ (2007) Seven steps in the evolution of the human imagination. In: Roth I (ed) Imaginative minds. Oxford University Press, Oxford, pp 3–29

Mithen SJ (2016) Imagination. New Scientist magazine

Morewedge CK, Huh YE, Vosgerau J (2010) Thought for food: imagined consumption reduces actual consumption. Science 330(6010):1530–1533

Mrazek MD, Smallwood J, Schooler JW (2012) Mindfulness and mind-wandering: Finding convergence through opposing constructs. Emotion 12:442–448

Mühlberger A, Wieser MJ, Kenntner-Mabiala R, Pauli P, Wiederhold BK (2007) Pain modulation during drives through cold and hot virtual environments. CyberPsychol Behav 10(4):516–522

Nardi BA (1993) A small matter of programming: perspectives on end user programming. MIT Press, Cambridge, MA

Newcomb E, Pashley T, Stasko J (2003) Mobile computing in the retail arena. In: Proceedings of CHI'2003, pp 337–344

Newell AF, Morgan ME, Gregor P, Carmichael A (2006) Theatre as an intermediary between users and CHI designers. In: Proceedings of CHI 2006. ACM Press, pp 111–117

Newell A, Simon HA (1972) Human problem solving. Prentice-Hall, Englewood Cliffs, NJ

Ngo DCL, Teo LS, Byrne JG (2003) Modelling interface aesthetics. Inf Sci 152:25–46

Nichols S, Stich S (2005) Mindreading: a cognitive theory of pretense. OUP

Nielsen J, Yssing C, Levinsen K, Clemmensen T, Ørngreen R, Nielsen L (2006) Embedding complementarity in hci methods and techniques – designing for the "cultural other". A working paper, Department of Informatics, Copenhagen Business School, pp 1–15

Norman DA, Draper SW (1986) User centered system design. Lawrence Erlbaum Associates, Hillsdale, NJ

Norman DA (1990) The design of everyday things. Doubleday, New York

Oatley K, Djikic M (2008) Writing as thinking. Rev Gen Psychol 12(1):9

Pascanu R, Li Y, Vinyals O, Heess N Buesing L, Racanière S, Reichert D, Webern T, Wierstra D, Battaglia P (2017) Learning model-based planning from scratch. arXiv preprint. arXiv:1707.06170

Peirce CS (1931–58) Collected papers (cp), vols 1–8. In: Hartshorne C, Weiss P, Burks AW (eds). Harvard University Press, Cambridge, MA. Electronic edition of J. Deely, Charlottesville, VA, Intelex

Pierson J, Jacobs A, Dreesen K, De Marez L (2008) Exploring and designing wireless city applications by way of archetype user research within a living lab. Observatorio (OBS*) J 5:099–118. http://obs.obercom.pt

Polkinghorne DE (1988) Narrative knowing and the human sciences. State University of New York Press, Albany

Popova YB (2015) Stories, meaning and experience. Routledge, New York

Postigo H (2008) Video game appropriation through modifications. Converg: Int J Res New Media Technol 14(1):59–74

Process Computers and Graphics 14(2):263–274

Pruit J, Grudin J (2003) Personas: practice and theory. In: Proceedings of the 2003 conference on designing for user experiences, pp 1–15

Pruitt J, Adlin T (2006) The persona lifecycle. Morgan Kaufmann, San Francisco, CA

Pylyshyn ZW (1973) What the mind's eye tells the mind's brain: a critique of mental imagery. Psychol Bull 80:1–24

Pylyshyn ZW (1981) The imagery debate: analogue versus tacit knowledge. Psychol Rev 86:383–394

Raskin J (1994) Intuitive equals familiar. Commun ACM 37(9):17

Reber R, Schwarz N, Winkielman P (2004) Processing fluency and aesthetic pleasure: Is beauty in the perceiver's processing experience? Pers Soc Psychol Rev 8(4):364–382

Reis S, Correia N (2011) An imaginary friend that connects with the user's emotions. In: Proceedings of the 8th international conference on advances in computer entertainment technology. ACM, p 1

Ribot T (1906) Essay on the creative imagination. Open Court, Chicago, IL

Ryan ML (2001) Narrative as virtual reality. immersion and interactivity in literature and electronic media. Johns Hopkins University Press, Baltimore

Sato S, Salvador T (1999) Methods & tools: playacting and focus troupes. Interactions, Sept–Oct 1999, p 35

Schacter DL, Tulving E (1994) Memory systems. MIT Press, Cambridge, MA

Schank RC, Abelson RP (1977) Goals, plans, scripts and understanding: an enquiry into human knowledge structures. Lawrence Erlbaum Associates

Scheffler I (1986) In praise of the cognitive emotions. In: Inquiries: philosophical studies of language, science, and learning. Hackett, Indianapolis, IN, pp 347–352

Schneider DJ (2004) The psychology of stereotyping. Guilford Press, New York

Schrepp M, Held T, Laugwitz B (2006) The influence of hedonic quality on the attractiveness of user interfaces of business management software. Interact Comput 18(5):1055–1069

Sharrock WW, Anderson RJ (1994) The user as a scenic feature of the design space. Des Stud 15(1):5–18

Simsarian KT (2003) Take it to the next stage: the roles of role playing in the design process. In: Ext. Abstracts CHI'2003, pp 1012–1013

Sinha RR (2003) Persona development for information-rich domains. In: CHI Extended Abstracts 2003, pp 830–831

Smith DC, Irby C, Kimball R, Verplank B, Harlsem E, Designing the star user interface. Byte 7(4):242–282

Smolucha L, Smolucha FC (1986) L.S. Vygotsky's theory of creative imagination. Paper presented xxx

Sparke P (1996) As long as it's pink; the sexual politics of taste. New York University Press

Steen M (2013) Co-design as a process of joint inquiry and imagination. Des Issues 29(2):16–28

Sternberg RJ, Lubart TI (1995) Defying the crowd: cultivating creativity in a culture of conformity. The Free Press, New York

Stuss, DT, Knight RT (eds) Function. Oxford University Press, pp 311–325

Suddendorf T, Corballis MC (1997) Mental time travel and the evolution of the human mind. Genet Soc Gen Psychol Monogr 123:133–167

Sutcliffe A (2003) Scenario-based requirements engineering. In: Proceedings of 11th IEEE international requirements engineering conference, Sept 2003. IEEE, pp 320–329

Suwa M, Tversky B (1997) What do architects and students perceive in their design sketches? Des Stud 18(4):385–403

Technology Strategy Board (2009) Mobile Phone security challenge. www.innovateuk.org.uk

The Linguistic Turn, Essays in Philosophical Method (1967) ed. by Richard M. Rorty, University of Chicago press, 1992, ISBN 978–0226725697 (an introduction and two retrospective essays)

The Psychology of Imagination: History, Theory and New Research Horizons (Niels Bohr Professorship Lectures in Cultural Psychology) Paperback – 23 Feb 2017 by Brady Wagoner (Author), Ignacio Bresco de Luna (Editor), & 1 more

Thomas NJ (1999) Are theories of imagery theories of imagination?: an active perception approach to conscious mental content. Cogn Sci 23(2):207–245

Tractinsky N, Katz AS, Ikar D (2000) What is beautiful is usable. Interact Comput 13(2):127–145

Tulving E (1983) Elements of episodic memory. Oxford University Press

Tulving E (2005) Episodic memory and autonoesis: uniquely human? In: Terrace HS, Metcalfe J (eds) The missing link in cognition: origins of self-reflective consciousness. Oxford University Press, pp 3–56

Turner, 2017 A psychology of UX. Springer

Turner S, Turner P (2003) Telling tales. Des Stud 24(6):537–547

Tversky A, Kahneman D (1973) Availability: a heuristic for judging frequency and probability. Cogn Psychol 5:207–202

Tversky B (2002) What do sketches say about thinking. In: 2002 AAAI spring symposium, sketch understanding workshop, Stanford University, AAAI Technical Report SS-02–08, pp 148–151

Van Leeuwen N (2011) Imagination is where the action is. J Philos cviii(2):55–77

van Oost E (2001) Materialized gender: how shavers configure the users' femininity and masculinity. In: Oudshoorn N, Pinch T (eds) How users matter. MIT Press, Cambridge, MA

Verstijnen IM, Hennessey JM et al (1998) Sketching and creative discovery. Des Stud 19(4):519–546

Vygotsky LS (1990) Imagination and creativity in childhood (trans Smolucha F) Sov Psychol 28(1):84–96 (Original work 1930)

Watson JB (1930) Behaviorism (revised edition). University of Chicago Press

Weber T, Racanière S, Reichert DP, Buesing L, Guez A, Rezende DJ, Badia AP et al (2017) Imagination-augmented agents for deep reinforcement learning. arXiv preprint. arXiv:1707. 06203

Wood L (2000) Brands and brand equity: definition and management. Manag Decis 38(9):662–669

Wong RY, Mulligan DK (2016) When a product is still fictional: anticipating and speculating futures through concept videos. In: Proceedings of the 2016 ACM conference on designing interactive systems, June 2016. ACM, pp 121–133

Zeki S (2009) Splendours and miseries of the brain. Wiley-Blackwell, Padstow, Cornwall, UK

Web Resources

Acting with technology: activity theory and interaction design. https://books.google.co.uk/ books?id=zCo3AgAAQBAJ&pg=PA217&dq=Wartofsky+tertiary+artefacts&hl=en&sa=X& ved=0ahUKEwj858Kk6pPZAhVICsAKHYkjC4gQ6AEITDAH#v=onepage&q=Wartofsky% 20tertiary%20artefacts&f=false

Amazon ref. https://www.amazon.com/Neil-Gaiman/e/B000AQ01G2/ref=pd_sim_14_bl_ 2/141–2680159-2733715?_encoding=UTF8&pd_rd_i=1840237422&pd_rd_r=2593a797- 9bf0-11e8-ba72-65e34763c523&pd_rd_w=YGFKl&pd_rd_wg=TkY7t&pf_rd_i=desktop- dp-sims&pf_rd_m=ATVPDKIKX0DER&pf_rd_p=2610440344683357453&pf_rd_r= SC6GGBWV8SHHHEB5705W&pf_rd_s=desktop-dp-sims&pf_rd_t=40701&refRID= SC6GGBWV8SHHHEB5705W

Bleeker J (2009) Design fiction: a short essay on design, science, fact and fiction. http://blog. nearfuturelaboratory.com/2009/03/17/design-fiction-a-short-essay-on-design-science-fact-and- fiction/

Brahic C (2014) Daydream believers: is imagination our greatest skill? New Scien- tist magazine. https://www.newscientist.com/article/mg22329870-400-daydream-believers-is- imagination-our-greatest-skill/#. VENtjouUcbh. Accessed 15 Dec 2017

Cartwright P, Noone L (2006) Critical imagination: a pedagogy for engaging pre-service teachers in the university classroom. College Q 9(4). Accessed 15 Feb 2012. http://www.senecac.on.ca/ quarterly/2006-vol09-num04fall/cartwright_noone.html. Accessed 15 Dec 2012

Colello SMG (2007) Imagination in children's writing: how high can fiction fly? http://www. hottopos.com/notand14/silvia.pdf. Accessed 11 Feb 2012

comScore (2009) comScore releases first Data on iPhone users in the U.K. http://www.comscore. com/Press_Events/Press_Releases/2009/3/UK_iPhone_Users. Accessed 12 Mar 2010

Descartes Mediations (first published 1641) https://books.google.co.uk/books/about/Descartes_ Meditations_on_First_Philosoph.html?id=yMwiTTpwasgC&redir_esc=y

Fitzgibbon A, Reiter E (2003) Memories for life: managing information over a human lifetime. www.memoriesforlife.org/document.php?id=14. Accessed 25 Sept 2019

Gaiman N (nd) Amazon ref. https://www.amazon.com/Neil-Gaiman/e/B000AQ01G2/ref=pd_ sim_14_bl_2/141–2680159-2733715?_encoding=UTF8&pd_rd_i=1840237422&pd_rd_r= 2593a797-9bf0-11e8-ba72-65e34763c523&pd_rd_w=YGFKl&pd_rd_wg=TkY7t&pf_rd_ i=desktop-dp-sims&pf_rd_m=ATVPDKIKX0DER&pf_rd_p=2610440344683357453&pf_ rd_r=SC6GGBWV8SHHHEB5705W&pf_rd_s=desktop-dp-sims&pf_rd_t=40701&refRID= SC6GGBWV8SHHHEB5705W

Google and BBC scrap VR projects. https://www.bbc.co.uk/news/technology-50080594

Hobbes T (1651) Leviathan. https://books.google.co.uk/books?id=YuBI1iaCw88C&printsec=
     frontcover&source=gbs_ge_summary_r&cad=0#v=onepage&q&f=false. Accessed 7 Oct 2018
http://medicine.exeter.ac.uk/research/healthresearch/cognitive-neurology/theeyesmind/
     conference/
http://www.sciencedirect.com/science/article/pii/S0747563208000733
http://www.usability.gov/how-to-and-tools/methods/system-usability-scale.html
https://books.google.co.uk/books?isbn=0262263424
https://books.google.co.uk/books?isbn=131729866
https://stanford.library.sydney.edu.au/archives/spr2012/entries/mental-imagery/
Jeremijenko N, How stuff is made project. www.howstuffismade.org/
Lamming M, Flynn M (1994) "Forget-me-not" intimate computing in support of human memory.
     In: Proceedings of FRIEND21 the international symposium on next generation human interface,
     Meguro Gajoen, Japan
"L.S. Vygotsky's Theory of Creative Imagination" Presented at 94th Annual Convention of the
     American Psychological Association at Washington, D.C., August, 1986 by Larry Smolucha,
     Shimer College Waukegan, Illinois and Francine C. Smolucha, University of Chicago
Ramachandran VS (2009) Self awareness: the last frontier. Edge Foundation web essay. www.edge.
     org/3rd_culture/rama08/rama08_index.html. Accessed 29 Dec 2012
science alert (2017) http://www.sciencealert.com/google-has-started-adding-imagination-to-its-
     deepmind-ai. Accessed 2018
Telegraph, Jan 2014. www.telegraph.co.uk/men/active/10568898/Sports-visualisation-how-to-
     imagine-your-way-to-success.html

Printed in the United States
By Bookmasters